A GUIDE TO COLLECTIONS ON PARAGUAY IN THE UNITED STATES

Recent Titles in
Reference Guides to Archival and Manuscript Sources
in World History

A Guide to Cuban Collections in the United States
Louis A. Pérez, Jr.

A Guide to Indian Manuscripts: Materials from Europe and North America
John F. Riddick, compiler

A Guide to Central American Collections in the United States
Thomas M. Leonard

A GUIDE TO COLLECTIONS ON PARAGUAY IN THE UNITED STATES

**Thomas Whigham
and Jerry W. Cooney**

Reference Guides to Archival
and Manuscript Sources in World History,
Number 4

Louis A. Pérez, Jr., Series Adviser

GREENWOOD PRESS
Westport, Connecticut • London

Library of Congress Cataloging-in-Publication Data

Whigham, Thomas.
    A guide to collections on Paraguay in the United States / Thomas
Whigham and Jerry W. Cooney.
      p. cm.—(Reference guides to archival and manuscript
sources in world history, ISSN 1054-9110 ; no. 4)
   Includes index.
   ISBN 0-313-29203-5 (alk. paper)
   1. Paraguay—History—Archival resources—Directories.
2. Manuscripts—United States—Facsimiles—Archival resources.
3. Archival resources—United States—Directories. I. Cooney,
Jerry W. (Jerry Wilson). II. Title. III. Series.
Z1821.W55 1995
[F2681]
016.9892—dc20   95-15449

British Library Cataloguing in Publication Data is available.

Library of Congress Catalog Card Number: 95-15449
ISBN: 0-313-29203-5
ISSN: 1054-9110

First published in 1995

Greenwood Press, 88 Post Road West, Westport, CT 06881
An imprint of Greenwood Publishing Group, Inc.

Printed in the United States of America

The paper used in this book complies with the
Permanent Paper Standard issued by the National
Information Standards Organization (Z39.48-1984).

10 9 8 7 6 5 4 3 2 1

A Arnaldo Manlio Fernández Benítez

Un buen amigo y guía conocedor al Paraguay

CONTENTS

Introduction   ix

Archives and Manuscripts

Arkansas   1

California   2

Connecticut   17

Georgia   18

Illinois   20

Indiana   22

Iowa   26

Kansas   28

Kentucky   35

Maine   37

Maryland   38

Massachusetts   41

Michigan   43

Minnesota   44

Mississippi   45

Missouri   46

New Jersey   50

New York   51

North Carolina   57

Ohio   59

Oregon   62

Rhode Island   63

Tennessee   64

Texas   65

Utah   70

Virginia   72

Washington, D. C.   73

West Virginia   100

Collection Index   101

Subject Index   107

INTRODUCTION

Few nations in the Western Hemisphere have been as remote from North American consciousness as the Republic of Paraguay. Even today, if one asked North Americans about this not-so-distant land, those who might have some knowledge of it (and who do not confuse it with Uruguay) would hesitantly mention Nazi refugees and old-fashioned military dictatorships. Even those scholars or businessmen with a general interest in Latin America will readily admit that, for them, Paraguay is basically terra incognita. They might know the general outlines of its tragic history of war and political repression. They might have heard of yerba mate, the traditional green tea drunk in every Paraguayan home. They might even have read of the enormous hydroelectric complexes that have been erected on Paraguay's rivers. But more than this they do not know.

       This lack of familiarity with Paraguay is hardly surprising. After all, the United States has had little human or commercial contact with that South American republic, certainly nothing comparable to that maintained with Mexico, the Caribbean states, or even Paraguay's larger neighbors, Brazil and Argentina. North American interest in Paraguay has instead been episodic in character. In the 1850s such entrepreneurs as Edward A. Hopkins sought bonanza fortunes there. Hopkins, who has gained a measure of notoriety, even infamy, in Paraguayan scholarly circles, went so far as to claim that Paraguay was the richest country in the New World after the United States. Yet, later in the same decade, United States relations with that country took such a dangerous turn that Washington even sent a naval flotilla up the Paraná River to force the Paraguayans to pay damages for an earlier incident.

       During the 1870s President Rutherford B. Hayes played a major role in Paraguayan history by acting as arbiter between the Asunción government and that of Argentina in a major land dispute. In the early twentieth century, a modest North American interest in investment in Paraguay developed, and relations with that republic, both directly and in the Pan American Union, became more important. In the 1930s, Washington offered its good offices in helping to bring to an end the war that had erupted with Bolivia over the Gran Chaco region. In the same decade the United States paid more attention to Asunción as the Good Neighbor Policy, and then Hemispheric

Solidarity, were developed. World War II, and then the Cold War, witnessed closer relations between the two nations, particularly during the first part of the long dictatorship of General Alfredo Stroessner (1954-1989). From the 1950s onward the United States has exercised a greater economic influence in Paraguay than previously, and particularly the North American cultural influence has been felt.

Even so, all too often United States interest in Paraguay has been passive or absentminded. So, too, has been the attention given to Paraguay by North American scholars, who treated the republic only in passing. Until the last generation North Americans wrote more novels about Paraguay than they did scholarly works. Indeed, until the 1980s, the number of specialists in the United States with real experience in, and knowledge of, Paraguay could be counted on a person's fingers. Nonetheless, by the 1980s a small, though highly dedicated, community of Paraguayanists had come into existence in the United States, mostly on university campuses. It has grown since that time and has successfully branched out, making useful contacts with colleagues in Europe, Argentina, Brazil, and, of course, in Paraguay itself. All of the scholarly disciplines have been involved in this development, from anthropology and political science to the natural and applied sciences and history.

The writing of this guide has to some extent been motivated by the appearance of this new community of Paraguayanists. At the same time, the guide clearly demonstrates that the road to Paraguayan studies is still wide open. Many fields and subjects related to Paraguay have yet to be effectively touched, and in the United States alone, a substantial base of documentary material is available to help initiate these new projects. It can only be hoped that young scholars, North American and otherwise, will find the many research opportunities tempting.

In the course of preparing this guide, we have consistently been surprised both with the quantity and quality of useful materials on Paraguay available in the United States. Historians in particular will be impressed with the various documentary collections. The Gondra materials at the University of Texas at Austin, for instance, are as valuable a source for Paraguay in the colonial period as anywhere in the world save perhaps for the Archivo General de Indias in Seville or the Archivo Nacional in Asunción. Late colonial and national era demographic materials are held in considerable volume at the Genealogical Society of Utah in Salt Lake City. And as for the twentieth century, the documents at the University of Kansas, and the various collections at the University of California at Riverside, cannot be equalled anywhere in the world, not even in Paraguay.

Missionary records make up a special, and almost untouched, category of documentary materials found in U.S. repositories. The collections of the various Mennonite archives are especially noteworthy in this respect (and perhaps even more so as records of the immigrant experience in Paraguay, the Mennonites being a key immigrant group in the Chaco during the present century).

Records of United States government agencies and departments make up another important category of useful documentary material. The National Archives are naturally a major source here, but many other government agencies maintain collections with documents on Paraguay. Taken as a whole, these materials are indispensable in any investigation on U.S.-Paraguayan relations, Paraguayan domestic politics and economics, and even such topics as trade conventions and hookworm eradication.

Given considerations of space, we have attempted to be as exhaustive as possible since no guide to Paraguayan sources in the United States has hitherto appeared. There have nonetheless been several categories of materials that we have made no systematic effort to cover, such an effort being beyond the scope of this guide; these categories include photographs, maps, and collections of newspapers, postcards, and memorabilia. We wish to express our appreciation to all the librarians, curators, and various Paraguayanists who took up their valuable time to address our many queries. In this respect, we wish to particularly mention Nancy Koller, Gayle Williams, Alexandra Mason, Diego Hay, Carolyn Autry, and Paul Brockman. We also wish to thank the Greenwood editorial staff who displayed great patience and understanding as we struggled to get the guide in publishable form. Any errors, omissions, or dubious inclusions are, of course, our sole responsibility.

ARCHIVES AND MANUSCRIPTS

ARKANSAS

University of Arkansas
Special Collections Division
University Libraries
Fayetteville, Arkansas 72701

1. Council for International Exchange of Scholars Records

These papers deal with the role of the CIES in educational exchange activities in higher education. CIES is a private agency that cooperates with the U.S. government in the administration of Fulbright scholar grants for advanced research and university teaching. Final reports of Americans and visiting scholars are included in this collection, as well as annual reports from Fulbright bi-national commissions and foundations, grant authorization lists, and log books regarding American scholars receiving awards under the Fulbright, Smith-Mundt, and Fulbright-Hays Acts. Latin America is represented in the more than 200 linear feet of records pertaining to this organization. Again, Paraguay is represented by materials scattered through these records. This collection is not completely processed so no guide yet exists.

2. U.S. Bureau of Educational and Cultural Affairs Historical Collection

This Bureau, formerly the Division of Cultural Relations of the United States State Department, was involved with the development of U.S. international educational and cultural exchange activities, including the Fulbright program. This collection contains diverse materials from the Fulbright and other exchange programs in Latin America, annual post reports on exchange activities, grantee lists for Americans and foreigners, statistics, country proposals, and general correspondence. Scattered throughout this collection is material pertaining to Paraguay. Unfortunately, no guide exists as the collection is yet not processed.

CALIFORNIA

University of California at Berkeley
Bancroft Library
Berkeley, California 94720

3. Lewis Winkler Bealer Papers

    Included in these papers is a biographical sketch of President José Félix Estigarribia. [Z-R 9]

4. George J. R. Gordon Report

    This report centered on commercial possibilities of Paraguay (written in Hampton Wick, 1843) and is a crucial, yet little-known item on the immediate post-Francia era; this microfilm copy was taken from the Public Records Office, London, Foreign Office documents (PRO-FO 13/302).

5. Various Papers, Manuscripts

    This collection contains some general papers relating to the Jesuit experience in South America, 1649-1757. Included in this case are letters from Bishop Palafox, 1649; from José de Barreda, Jesuit Provincial of Paraguay, 1753; and from Alvaro Cienfuegos, Jesuit Cardinal, 1721; as well as a file containing one report, 1757, on a reputed plan to establish a Jesuit republic in Paraguay. [M-M 1755]

6. Society of Jesus Papers (I)

These papers are made up of 146 microfilm exposures of documents on the Jesuit experience in Brazil, Paraguay, and Uruguay, 1634-1669; the originals of these documents, which include letters, *cartas anúas*, and other reports, are found in the Biblioteca Nacional, Rio de Janeiro. [Z-D III]

7. Society of Jesus Papers (II)

This collection contains 475 pages of hand-copied documents relating to the Jesuits in the Indies, 1605?-1753; these documents contain various letters, verses, and notes of protest and criticism. Two items deal specifically with Paraguay:

> 1. Barreda, José de. Memorial que . . . presentó al señor comisario Marqués de Valde-Lirios . . . Córdoba, Argentina, 19 July 1753, 35 pp. (plea addressed by the Jesuit Provincial of Paraguay requesting indulgence for the Indians in the Jesuit missions who have failed to comply with the royal order for migration, based on the 1750 Treaty of Madrid that ceded their lands to the Portuguese).

> 2. Motibos que alegan los Yndios del Paraguay para no hacer la trasmigración a otras tierras . . . Asunción?, 1753?, 38 pp. (summary of the explanation addressed by the Indians of the Jesuits missions of Paraguay to the Governor of Buenos Aires concerning their failure to obey the evacuation order; and petition asking that their case be laid before the King so that the Indians should not be treated as rebels. [M-M 1744]

Center for Mennonite Brethren Studies
4824 East Butler Avenue
Fresno, California 93727

8. General Conference of Mennonite Brethren Churches Board of General Welfare and Public Relations Records

This Record Group A 260 contains material on the various North American agencies of the Mennonite Brethren that aided in the resettlement of Mennonite refugees from Canada or Europe after World War I, and the repeat of that immigration from Europe after World War II, covering the years 1934 to 1967. Much of its activities in both instances was warding off famine in Europe. Reports from workers in Paraguay are included. The strongest period of concentration is the 1950s through 1960s. This group is divided into four series: I. Minutes, 1937-1967. II. Correspondence, 1940-1967. III. Financial Records, 1934-1967. IV. Other material, 1940-1967. Series II has three subseries: I. P.C. Hiebert correspondence, 1940-1958. II. M.A. Kroeker correspondence, 1954-1967. III. Correspondence of other board members and staff persons, 1955-1967. All the minutes through 1943 are in German with a typewritten English translation. Most of the other correspondence is in German.

9. Gerhard B. Giesbrecht Papers

Gerhard B. Giesbrecht was a Russian Mennonite immigrant to Paraguay in the 1920s. In Paraguay he worked as a school teacher in a Mennonite Colony and then as a missionary to the Chaco Indians. This collection (Record Group M 61) contains personal correspondence, a diary for the years 1937-1938, and sermons. Most material is in German.

10. Licht den Indianern. Records

Within this Record Group GC 232 are the accounts of the Mennonite missionary activity among the Indians of the Gran Chaco for the years 1935-1987. Minutes of the bodies involved, reports, correspondence and Indian language publications are found here. Most of the material is also in German. Since most of the material came to the Center as part of the Gerhard B. Giesbrecht Papers (Record Group M61) and then was winnowed out from personal papers, it might be wise for researchers also to consult the Geisbrecht collection.

11. Mennonite Brethren Missions/Services, Paraguay Mission Records

In this Record Group A 250, Subgroup 11 is material on the Mennonite's missions to the various Chaco Indian peoples for the period 1931-1983. Included are minutes of the various agencies involved, reports, correspondence, historical accounts, publications, news releases, financial reports, and maps. Most of the material is in German.

12. Gerhard Ratzlaff Collection

Gerhard Ratzlaff (1927-1969), a native of Paraguay, attended school in the United States at California State University, Fresno, where he wrote an 1974 M.A. thesis titled "An Historical- Political Study of the Mennonites in Paraguay." That thesis is greatly concerned with the involvement of Paraguayan Mennonites with National Socialism in that country during the 1930s and 1940s. Mr. Ratzlaff left historical documents collected during his research to the Center (Record Group M 51). All items in this collection are photocopies and most are in German.

The Mennonite Brethren Center has excellent guides to the above collections, and there are generally no restrictions on the use of the Center's materials.

The Huntington Library
Department of Manuscripts
1151 Oxford Road
San Marino, California 91108

13. Huntington Library Department of Manuscripts

The Huntington Library possesses only a few manuscripts in reference to Paraguay. There are several letters relative to the Jesuit Missions in the 1750s and 1760s, one by Joseph Cardile to Francisco Baptista, 26 Setiembre de 1756 and the other by Andrés Marcos Buriel to Juan Baltasar of 20 Juliode 1760.

14. Willis Collection

Within this collection is some casual correspondence of October, 1912, touching upon some Paraguayan themes.

National Archives
Pacific Southwest Region
24000 Avila Road
Laguna Miguel, California 92677

15. Vice President Richard M. Nixon Papers

Within this regional depository are the papers relating to Vice-President Nixon's official visit to Paraguay in 1958.

The Richard M. Nixon Library & Birthplace
18001 Yorba Linda Boulevard
Yorba Linda, California 92686

16. Richard Nixon Papers

As of 1994 many of Richard Nixon's papers have not yet been deposited in this library. Those that have that pertain to Paraguay are in the Pre-Presidential Papers Series (PPS) File 320, Folder 75 "Paraguay," and deal, for the most part, with routine diplomatic courtesy. They are open to researchers.

Ronald Reagan Library
40 Presidential Drive
Simi Valley, California 93065

17. Ronald Reagan Papers

As one might imagine, as of 1994 almost all the records pertaining to Paraguay in the Reagan Library have not yet been processed and are unavailable to the researcher. Those that some day will be of interest are found in the White House Office of Records Management (WHORM): Subject File, Country 123 - Paraguay, and in the same series, Foreign Affairs: Diplomatic Affairs - Consular Relations FO002. Scattered about in other WHORM subject Files is material relating to Paraguay in such diverse files as narcotics, trade and tariffs, Peace Corps, etc.

In the White House Staff and Office Collections under Roger Fontaine, there are files in box 90110 Paraguay, box 90122 Paraguay, and box 90128 Paraguay, all, of course, unprocessed. In the Records of the Latin American Affairs Director of the National Security Council there are also five boxes labeled Paraguay under the numerical designations 90512, 92376, 92352, 91717, and 91718. Records of the Office of the Assistant to the President for National Security Affairs many be found under Country File - box 91371 Paraguay, Volume One 1/20/81-1/20/85. Furthermore, under Lilac, Robert H. there exists Files - box 90330 AT Paraguay (1/1/81); and under Wiggs, David C. : Files - box 96698 Paraguay. Some time will pass before the above material is available to the public.

University of California at Riverside
The Tomás Rivera Library
Riverside, California 92517

The University of California Riverside Library boasts the strongest collection of Paraguayan primary materials of any institution on the West Coast. Obtained through the efforts of Hugo Rodríguez Alcalá and others, the materials cover a wide variety of subjects and are especially valuable for the 1890-1925 and 1954-1989 periods. Any analysis of Paraguayan intellectual elites, their composition, values, and impact on national life, would greatly benefit from a perusal of these documents, as would any study of twentieth-century revolutionary movements. The UCR collections could also form the documentary base for biographical studies or investigations into Paraguayan family history.

The Latin American Studies program at the university has published a helpful research guide for a small portion of the various collections —Pastora Montero de López Román, et al, *Research Guide to the Godoi Díaz-Pérez Collection in the Library of the University of California Riverside* (Riverside: Latin American Studies Research Guide No. 1, 1973). Unfortunately, the guide is rather selective and should be complemented by Araxie P. Churukian, "The Juan Silvano Godoi Collection at the University of California, Riverside," *Latin American Research Review*, 27:1 (1991), pp. 121-124. Even so, a researcher may encounter difficulties since, with few exceptions, the Riverside holdings remain unorganized and uncatalogued and therefore represent a major challenge. If mined assiduously, however, they should yield some substantial finds. Access to the documents is permitted at the Special Collections Department during regular library hours and photocopying is generally permitted.

18. Viriato Díaz Pérez Collection

The U.C.R. Library also houses the personal papers of Viriato Díaz Pérez (1875-1958), a Spanish author and critic who immigrated to Paraguay in 1905. One year later he was named director of the National Library and from that point on played various important roles in Paraguayan academic and intellectual life. A prolific writer, Díaz Pérez produced many works on theosophical themes as well as poetry, history, and literary criticism. The U.C.R. holdings include several as-yet unorganized boxes of his personal correspondence. Selected newspaper clippings and review articles, manuscripts, personal memorabilia, and some issues of journals (caja 26 has a few numbers of *El Economista Paraguayo*) complete the collection. The Viriato Díaz Pérez papers are stored together with those of his father, Nicolás Díaz Pérez, an Extremaduran journalist and literary figure who died before his son left for Paraguay. Though the materials of neither man have been adequately catalogued, the diligent researcher will doubtlessly find in them many intriguing items on modern Paraguay.

19. Julio César Chaves Collection

In 1971 U.C.R. purchased more than thirty-three hundred volumes from the library of Julio César Chaves (1909-1988), the emminent biographer of Dr. José Gaspar de Francia and Carlos Antonio López. Although the U.C.R. holdings include no personal correspondence of Chaves, they contain a large number of pamphlets (many detailing the 1932-1935 Chaco dispute) and secondary works. No primary documentation is included, an interesting exception being a bound series of letters (probably contemporary copies) from Carlos Antonio López and Francisco Solano López to their agent in London, Carlos Calvo. Written between 1860 and 1862, the letters are cataloged at Riverside as Special Collections Mss. 36.

20. Juan Silvano Godoi Collection

Juan Silvano Godoi (1850-1926) was a key figure in the political and intellectual life of Paraguay in the complicated period following the Triple Alliance War. As a young man, he served in the 1870 Constituent Assembly, which framed the national constitution that remained in force until 1940. He later served in the National Congress and acted as Paraguayan Minister to Brazil before beginning a long, though very active, exile in Buenos Aires. During the 1880s he was at the center of several Liberal Party plots designed to wrest control of the Paraguayan state from the ruling Colorados. The latter group ultimately granted him an amnesty and he returned to Asunción in 1895 to become Director of the National Library, Museum, and Archive, a post he held for the rest of his life. During his years in exile, Godoi assembled an award-winning collection of art and over 20,000 books with which he formed the nucleus of the National Library. Though the books have been largely dispersed since the 1930s, his collection of artwork is still maintained on public display at the Museum of Fine Art in Asunción.

Godoi witnessed first-hand the cycle of golpes and intrigues that characterized the postwar years. His own political career, moreover, coincided exactly with the earliest phase of Colorado-Liberal rivalry, a period that is only just now coming under scholarly scrutiny. When he died at the age of seventy-five, he left behind an important collection of letters, manuscripts, clippings, memorabilia, and personal diaries.

This collection was purchased by UCR in 1968. Thirteen years later Professor Thomas Whigham gave it a preliminary arrangement by category; this organization, together with Whigham's annotations, have been retained until the present and are the basis for a computerized listing (prepared in dBase III Plus) available to users. The Godoi materials themselves are stored in twenty acid-free boxes in the Special Collections Department of the UCR Library.

Box I holds manuscripts of articles, essays, and speeches written by Godoi. Here, for example, we encounter a 1913(?) article on the Chaco question (in which Godoi recommends a mixed commission be established to resolve the border dispute); a satirical piece called the "República de San Marino: historia de un majistrado celebre;" speeches recounting the deeds of José Eduvigis Díaz, Antonio José de Sucre, and Justo José de Urquiza; and an 1889 testimonial honoring the people of Corrientes, Argentina.

Boxes 2 and 3 contain Godoi's personal diaries. These ten volumes of "Aconteci-mientos históricos, políticos, personales y familiares" may constitute the most valuable piece in the entire collection, seeing as they cover the entire critical period from 13 January 1897 to 31 January 1921. Regrettably, volume five, which covers the pivotal year of 1904, appears to be missing from the collection.

Boxes 4, 5, and 6 contain letters sent to Godoi from prominent political and literary figures. The correspondents include controversial historian and diplomat Alejandro Audibert, author of several key scholarly works on Paraguayan border disputes; sports figure Pacífico de Ayala, president of Asunción's best-known soccer organization in the early 1920s; Legionario officer Federico Guillermo Báez, who sided with Argentina against Paraguay in the Triple Alliance conflict and went on to fill several key political posts in the 1870s; Argentine historian Ramón J. Cárcano, whose incisive treatment of the Triple Alliance War is still widely read; Rodolfo Chodasewicz, who introduced European engineering standards to the Argentine army during the 1864-1870 war; Hector Francisco Decoud, author of several critical works on the Solano López period; revolutionary leader Nicanor Godoi, Juan Silvano's brother and the assassin, in 1877, of Paraguayan president Juan Bautista Gill; Juan E. O'Leary, revisionist historian, polemicist, and rehabilitator of Marshal Francisco Solano López; and Estanislao Zeballos, Argentine author and Minister of Culture.

Godoi's own letters (originals, copies, and early drafts) are contained in Box 7. Some examples are a 1907 note to Bishop Juan Sinforiano Bogarín; an 1893 letter to Colorado politician José Segundo Decoud regarding the purchase of armaments; an 1899 missive to Uruguayan president Julio Herrera y Obes in which Godoi discusses the significance of Gladstone, Bismarck, and Thiers; letters to Benigno Ferreira and Cecilio Báez, Liberal Party leaders during the first decade of the twentieth century; and many notes to Godoi's wife and family members.

Boxes 8 and 9 contain miscellaneous correspondence between third parties. Here, for instance, we see an 1873 letter from Candido Bareiro to Bernardino Caballero (both of whom later became president) noting the arrival of horses and other "elements"; a letter of October 1807 from landowner and militia officer Manuel Atanasio Cabañas to merchant Salvador Doldan regarding a shipment of 84 tercios of yerba mate; a pre-1814(?) letter sent by Dr. José Gaspar de Francia to merchant Florencio Antonio Zelada; an appeal sent at the beginning of the Triple Alliance War by Paraguayan diplomat José Rufo Caminos to Treasury Minister Mariano González asking for assistance in maintaining the consulate at the Argentine city of Paraná; and one very moving 1868 missive written by Juan Francisco López, son of the Marshal, to his mother, Eliza Alicia Lynch, thanking her for an unexpected gift of chocolate (the young man, who was only in his teens, died two years later at Cerro Cora, during the last engagement of the war).

Box 10 holds miscellaneous materials pertaining to Godoi's career. These include calling cards, invitations, photos, wine labels, newspaper clippings, receipts for armaments and personal expenses, dedicatory poems, and even a map of the Río Tebicuary-mí. Similar materials on the careers of such individuals as Argentine historian Antonio Zinny, Paraguayan bibliophile Enrique Solano López, and Chilean intellectual Rómulo Mundiola are seen in Box 11.

Boxes 12 and 13 contain handwritten copies of archival documents, the great majority evidently taken from the Archivo Nacional de Asunción (an institution headed by Godoi in the first decades of the twentieth century). These copies may be of great importance because it is not at all clear that the originals still exist in Paraguay. Included here are copies of all documents listed under Letter "C" of the Sección Civil of the Archivo; genealogical records dealing with María de Trejo y Sanabria; several documents on the 1865 Uruguayana campaign; various commercial treaties between Paraguay and other states; 45 documents on the career of José Gervasio Artigas; a selection of letters of Dr. Francia dealing with French botanist Aimé Bonpland; and a copy of the last will and testament of Petrona Recalde Rodríguez de Francia.

Boxes 14 and 15 hold legal and political documents, most of which are archival copies though some of which are originals. Highlights here include various several eighteenth-century letters of a commercial nature written by Florencio Antonio Zelada and Pedro Nolasco Domecque; a series of decrees and proclamations of Carlos Antonio López; several discourses by the Argentine and Brazilian ministers to Paraguay regarding the establishment of a provisional regime in 1869; an 1871 "State of the Union" message of President Cirilo Antonio Rivarola; 30 miscellaneous documents dealing with the 1873 revolution (including notes from Juan B. Egusquiza, José Acosta, and José Dolores Molas); proclamations of Higínio Uriarte and Bernardino Caballero (1870s and 80s); and a quantity of documents, some written in code, detailing Godoi's participation in plots to overthrow the Paraguayan government in the late 1870s.

Box 16 holds a miscellany of materials on the efforts of Eliza Alicia Lynch to recover lands and properties once granted her by Marshal Francisco Solano López. These documents, crucial to any understanding of the Marshal's government, are almost certainly unique.

Financial documents, receipts, and tally sheets are the focus of Box 17. Here, for example, are documents relating to the Comité Paraguayo's attempts to gain loans in London in the 1880s; and materials detailing land transfers by the López family and others during the same decade.

Boxes 18 and 19 contain newspapers and newspaper clippings dealing with Paraguayan politics and social life. They are especially useful for an examination of Paraguayan cultural and literary trends in the 1920s.

Box 20 holds miscellaneous materials, including a collection of Paraguayan banknotes (1850s and 1860s); a funeral notice; minutes of an 1889 meeting of the Comité Paraguayo; a Paraguayan masonic document; various poems and short essays by Godoi and others; and a series of eulogies written to honor Silvio Pettirossi, the "father of Paraguayan aviation," who died in a plane crash in Buenos Aires in 1915.

21. Miscellaneous Holdings-UCR

The Special Collections Library at UCR boasts a valuable collection of eighteenth-century imprints on the Jesuits in Paraguay. Aside from the Jesuit materials, the Special Collections Library also possesses a massive twelve-volume collection of typed, hand-corrected materials assembled by a participant in the Chaco Peace Conference of 1935-1939 that includes all relevant protocols and documentation; and two typed copies of an informative Spanish-language report on Paraguayan nutritional problems submitted in 1946 to the U.S. Office of Inter-American Affairs, Food Supply Division. In addition, the Special Collections Library boasts an early complete reprint of the 1840s-1850s periodical *El Paraguayo Independiente* as well as some unusual books and pamphlets on nineteenth and early twentieth-century Paraguay. The general collection at the UCR Library should not go unrecognized insofar as its Paraguay holdings are concerned. The importance of the Tomás Rivera Library for students of Paraguay can be seen by reference to the number of volumes it holds; UCR possesses over 200 titles on the Chaco War, and another 280 on the Guaraní Indians and language. Possibly the most important items in the open stacks, however, are copies of two collections of typed transcripts of documents from the Archivo Nacional de Asunción, one concentrating on the Dr. Francia years (6 vols.) and the other on the Carlos Antonio López years (10 vols.); the original transcripts make up part of the Natalicio González Collection at the University of Kansas.

22. Hugo Rodríguez Alcalá Collection

Between 1974 and 1980 noted Paraguayan poet and essayist Hugo Rodríguez Alcalá made a series of generous donations to U.C.R. Library from his private collection of letters and literary memorabilia. The collection is in every way an excellent source for biographers, critics, and literary historians of modern Paraguay as it touches on nearly every important Paraguayan writer of the present century. Among its holdings, one can encounter:

1. Letters of Augusto Roa Bastos 30 letters (48 leaves), typescript, signed by the author, to Hugo Rodríguez Alcalá. 3 short stories by Roa Bastos (18 leaves), typescript. Typescript article (25 leaves) regarding Roa Bastos by H. Rodríguez Alcalá. Miscellaneous articles (excerpts and offprints) on Roa Bastos (25 separate items).

2. Letters of Gabriel Casaccia (bound in one volume); 26 letters (78 leaves), typescript, signed by the author (including 3 letters laid in and unbound) to Hugo Rodríguez Alcalá. 2 letters from Pablo Max Ynsfrán regarding Casaccia, typescript, signed. 5 carbon copies or photocopies of letters by Casaccia. Manuscript article by Josefina Plá on Casaccia's *Los exiliados.* Letter, manuscript, signed, from Paraguayan historian Efraím Cardozo to Hugo Rodríguez Alcalá, concerning Casaccia's work. 6 miscellaneous articles, printed, on Casaccia, along with various notes on the author's career. Typescripts of letters and reprints of critical articles (71 leaves), including 9 typescript copies of letters from Casaccia to his brother.

3. Memorabilia of poet Alejandro Guanes (1872-1925) — 52 items, High School documents, letters written by Paraguayan historians who were contemporaries of Guanes, two photographs, and several printed pieces.

4. Letters and publications of Spanish-born poet Josefina Plá 8 letters from Pla to H. Rodríguez Alcalá, 1949-1963. 18 publications (poems and newspaper pieces) by Plá, 1942-1968.

5. 3 letters of poet Herib Campos Cervera to H. Rodríguez Alcalá, 1949-1953.

6. 9 letters of historian Justo Pastor Benítez to H. Rodríguez Alcalá, 1958-1961.

7. 14 letters of Rubén Bareiro Saguier to H. Rodríguez Alcalá, 1967-1978.

8. 8 letters of poet Elvio Romero to H. Rodríguez Alcalá, 1953-1957.

9. 20 letters of historian Efraím Cardozo to H. Rodríguez Alcalá, 1968-1971.

10. 40 letters of historian Pablo Max Ynsfrán to H. Rodríguez Alcalá, 1962-1970.

11. 53 letters of Teresa Lamas Carísimo de Rodríguez Alcalá to H. Rodríguez Alcalá, 1962-1971.

In addition to this rich harvest of primary documentation on Paraguayan literature, the Rodríguez Alcalá materials also include substantial correspondence with Spanish and Argentine literary figures such as Ricardo Güiraldes, Alejandro Korn, Americo Castro, Francisco Romero, Francisco Ayala, and the Nobel Prize winner, Camilo José Cela. The collection also contains hundreds of pamphlets, newspaper clippings, offprints, autographs, typescripts, pictures and prints, all relating to modern Paraguay's place within the Hispanic literary and cultural tradition.

23. Guillermo Arturo Weyer Political Archive

This collection, obtained by UCR in 1992, consists of the entire library and political archive of the Agencia Noticiosa Paraguaya, a news agency that operated in Buenos Aires from 1973 until it was closed by the Argentine military regime in 1977 and again from 1984 until the fall of General Alfredo Stroessner in 1989. Compiled over a thirty-year period by Guillermo Arturo Weyer, director of the ANP, the Archivo is unique in the United States in that it focuses on the activities of modern Paraguayan opposition parties and organizations, many of them clandestine. It includes books, pamphlets, newspaper clippings, and thousands of documents from political, labor, peasant, student, and guerrilla organizations. The Partido Revolucionario Febrerista, Partido Comunista Paraguayo, and Movimiento Popular Colorado are particularly well represented.

It is difficult to briefly summarize the holdings of such a massive collection. As of this writing, moreover, it has yet to be completely inventoried and it seems clear that a portion of the Archivo was lost in transit from Buenos Aires. Scholars will nevertheless appreciate the breadth and variety of the materials that U.C.R. has obtained in this collection from the following, rather abbreviated description.

The strength of the Archivo Político lies in its documents section, which is organized into thirteen categories: (A) Partidos Políticos Paraguayos (en el Paraguay, en el exilio, y en la clandestinidad); (B) Movimientos, Agrupaciones, Frentes Políticos; (C)

Organizaciones y Grupos Guerrilleros; (D) Organizaciones Sindicales; (E) Organizaciones Campesinas; (F) Movimientos, Centros y Federaciones de Estudiantes; (G) Organizaciones de Defensa de los Derechos Humanos y de Solidaridad con las Luchas Populares; (H) Agrupaciones Femeninas; (I) Otras Agrupaciones del Exilio; (J)

Iglesia Católica; (K) Instituciones Privadas de Información e Investigación; (L) Publicaciones Periodisticas Varias, and; (M) Publicaciones Políticas y Publicaciones Varias.

Within Category A of the documents section one encounters various letters, reports, and manifestos of Colonel Rafael Franco, former president and leader of the Febrerista movement in exile (1940s-50s). One also encounters resolutions and reports of the Central Committee of Paraguay's Communist Party (1930s-60s), as well as a wealth of *boletines* and periodical publications of the PCP, Febrerista Party, MOPOCO and its associated organizations, the Liberal Party in Exile, and the Christian Democratic Party. Category A also contains a substantial collection of documents from the governing Colorado Party that detail the Stroessner regime's approach and attitude towards opposition groups.

Category B boasts an impressive compilation of documents and periodical publications of Paraguayan exile groups operating in Buenos Aires, Montevideo, Madrid, and such curious locations as Oslo, Leningrad, Athens, and New Delhi. Of particular interest are several items from the 1970s Agrupación Revolucionaria de Trabajadores, the first major organization of Paraguayan Trotskyists (associated with Argentina's Socialist Workers Party).

Category C focuses on documents drawn from Paraguayan guerrilla organizations, and in this regard, it is perhaps the most intriguing category in the entire Archivo Político. Some materials of the late 1950s-early 1960s Frente Unido de Liberación Nacional and the Movimiento de Liberación Nacional "14 de Mayo" are present as are items from the mid-1970s Organización Primero de Marzo. All three organizations were ultimately destroyed by the repressive apparatus of General Stroessner. Unfortunately for the researcher, it appears that a portion of the documents meant for this category never arrived from South America, though they do appear in the Archivo's finding guide. Perhaps when U.C. Riverside completes its inventory of the collection these documents will be recovered.

Labor union materials, both from exile groups and groups working in Paraguay, are contained in Category D. In this case, noteworthy documents come from the Confederación Paraguaya de Trabajadores, a Montevideo-based association of radical trade unionists that had regrouped in Uruguay after the disastrous general strike in Asunción in 1958. Another useful item is a sizable *carpeta* with notes, communications, and various materials of that faction of the C.P.T. that had remained behind to cooperate with the Stroessner government (1958-1970).

Category E pertains to Peasant Organizations. As with some of the other materials, the category evidently did not arrive complete from South America; in its present state, it boasts only a few papers from the Servicio Arquidiocesano de Comercialización.

Student organizations are the focus of Category F. Noteworthy in this case is considerable documentation from associations of Paraguayan students at Argentine universities.

Category G deals with documents from Paraguayan Human Rights organizations. As the few items included here demonstrate, most of these groups necessarily worked from exile through 1989. They were influential, however, in concentrating world opinion on improving human rights conditions in Stroessner's Paraguay.

Category H boasts a few items from Paraguayan women's organizations, notably the Unión de Mujeres Paraguayas and the Frente Amplio de Mujeres (1960s-80s).

Category I has a few miscellaneous papers from the Club Atlético Deportivo Paraguayo of Buenos Aires (early 1980s). The finding guide lists two other groups in this miscellaneous category, but their papers never arrived at U.C.R.

Several minor items from Paraguay's Roman Catholic Church make up Category J, notably a declaration by opposition priests on Stroessner's visit to Buenos Aires in 1972, and a collection of bound volumes of *Comunidad* (1960s) and *Sendero* (1970s and 80s), both publications of the Conferencia Episcopal Paraguaya. Category K covers materials from private institutes and "think-tanks" in Paraguay. The various publications of the Banco Paraguayo de Datos (late 1970s through early 1980s) are particularly important here.

Category L contains periodical publications used over the years by the Agencia Noticiosa Paraguaya staff. This is a very large category (a marginal inscription in the finding guide states that one portion alone amounts to 320 kilograms of paper). Category M contains miscellaneous publications, mostly of a political nature. Finally, some uncatalogued materials have made their way into the Weyer collection. These include a file of manuscript materials of the dramatist Alcibiades González Delvalle; a file on 1978 Asunción chess tournaments; and two large files of photocopies from the FBI and U.S. State Department, the first dealing with Nazi espionage in Paraguay during the early 1940s, and the second focusing on the 1947 civil war.

San Diego State University
Malcolm A. Love Library
San Diego, California 92182

24. Abraham P. Nasatir Collection

Abraham Nasatir was a well-known historian of Latin American and borderlands history and professor at San Diego State University for fifty years beginning in 1928. Aside from his many scholarly activities, Nasatir was involved in consular work in San Diego and from 1936 to 1951 acted as vice consul for Paraguay in that southern California city. After his death in 1991 his personal papers were transferred to the Special Collections Department of the SDSU Library. The Nasatir Collection, which is housed in five large boxes (B 301-305), consists of correspondence, research papers, bibliographies, book reviews, speeches, teaching and consular materials, and personal miscellany.

Those interested in the Paraguayan consular documents should pay particular attention to Box 3, nos. 16 and 17. Some additional correspondence dealing with Nasatir's consular activities can apparently be found in the other boxes (although locating exactly where might be difficult because a full two boxes represent papers salvaged from a 1985 fire at the professor's home and are presumably damaged).

25. Love Library — Special Collections Department

In the Love Library is a rare *Colección de documentos oficiales; transcripciones, manifestaciones, declaraciones, papeles tomados a López en el asalto de 27 de diciembre de de 1868* . . . (np, 1869?).

CONNECTICUT

Yale University
Sterling Memorial Library
New Haven, Connecticut 06520

26. David Curtis DeForest Papers

These papers cover the latter's career as a U.S.-born merchant, privateer, and diplomat in Argentina during the earliest stages of that country's national period. There are a few minor references to Paraguay in several letters.

27. Emmons Family Papers

This collection comprises the private letters, scrapbooks, and official correspondence of George Foster Emmons (1811-1882), a career U.S. naval officer who commanded the Frigate *Savannah* off the South American coast at the time of the *Water Witch* incident.

28. James Watson Webb Papers

This material covers the period of this diplomat's service as U.S. minister to the court of Dom Pedro II from 1861 to 1865; Webb was present in Rio de Janeiro during the first year of the war with Paraguay and his notes touch periodically on that conflict (especially on the touchy question of Brazil's impressment of American seamen into the Guarda Nacional).

GEORGIA

Jimmy Carter Library
One Copenhill Avenue
Atlanta, Georgia 30307

29. Jimmy Carter Papers

Within the Carter Library, open to researchers, is the White House Central file, Subject File Country 123 - Paraguay, in Box CO - 49. Most documents in this file pertaining to Paraguay are of a routine diplomatic nature. The same holds true for White House Central File, Subject File, Foreign Affairs 2 (Diplomatic - Consular Relations) Country 123 in Box FO - 10. Diplomatic messages from Paraguay are found in the White House Central file, Subject File, Messages 1, Country 123 - Paraguay, Box ME -15. Scattered throughout other White House Central Files, dealing with such matters as the OAS, the Pan American Health Organization, etc., are references to Paraguay. The library possesses excellent cross reference aids to pursue topics among these files.

In the Files of the White House Counsel's Office, there is a folder titled "Letelier, Orlando," 11/79 in Box 98. That folder may shed some light on the peripheral role that Paraguay, or rather President Stroessner, played in this matter.

In the files of Peter Bourne, Special Assistant to the President for Health Issues, there is a folder "Paraguay" in Box 42. That Special Assistant was deeply concerned with the traffic in narcotics from Latin America, and the material in this folder may be of interest to those delving into Paraguay's involvement in the drug trade.

As of 1994 only about one third of the Carter White House Files are available to researchers. And unfortunately, the files of National Security Advisor Zbigniew Brzezinski and his staff are not yet open.

University of Georgia
Ilah Dunlap Little Memorial Library
Athens, Georgia 30602

30. Archivo Nacional de Asunción

The Ilah Dunlap Little Memorial Library at the University of Georgia, like that of U.C. Riverside and U.C. Los Angeles, boasts a photocopied ten-volume collection of typescript archival documents on Dr. Francia the originals of which can be found in the Natalicio González Collection at the Spencer Research Library, University of Kansas.

ILLINOIS

University of Illinois Urbana Champlain
Main Library
Urbana Champlain, Illinois 61801

31. Albert Barlow Hale Collection

The Library at the University of Illinois-Urbana Champlain owns one small collection of documents on Paraguay that was compiled by Albert Barlow Hale, once an instructor of ophthalmology at the university. The documents concern his work as a commercial attaché in the Platine republics between 1914 and 1916. The Hale Collection is stored at the Library's archive.

Loyola University Chicago
University Archives
6525 North Sheridan Road
Chicago, Illinois 60626

32. Institute of Jesuit History

In the early part of this century Loyola University maintained an Institute of Jesuit History which flourished until the mid-1950s and then gradually faded away. During its lifetime it collected documents in the photostat form on all aspects of Jesuit history, the activities of this order in the Río de la Plata included. Unfortunately, the key to this collection was destroyed and therefore documents within the collection are exceedingly hard to locate.

33. Rare Jesuitica Collection

The university archives also contain the Collection of Rare Jesuitica. Here one finds rare books on Jesuit activities throughout the world, as well as selected documents. Various books and documents refer to the activities of Jesuits in Paraguay. Works by Pierre Francois Xavier de Charlevoix, Martin Dobrizhoffer, Ludovico Antonio Muratori, and others are found here as well as various documents such as "Decreto de la magestad del rey catholico Phelipe V. sobre varias acusaciones dadas en su real consejo contra los jesuitas del Paraguay. ... 1744," and "Noticias de el estado de la provincia del paraguay, venidas por Buenos-Ayres con cartas de 20. de febrero de 1733."

INDIANA

David W. Dennis
610 West Main Street
Richmond, Indiana 47374

34. William C. Dennis Papers

Mr. Dennis has in his possession the papers of William C. Dennis (1878-1962). As a State Department solicitor, the latter Dennis was at one time involved in Paraguayan boundary arbitration. The Lilly Library of Richmond, Indiana states that in the future they may receive those papers.

DePauw University
Archives and Special Collections (Indiana United Methodism)
Roy O. West Library
Greencastle, Indiana 46135

35. Thomas Bond Wood Papers

DePauw University holds the papers of Thomas Bond Wood, a prominent Methodist missionary to the Río de Plata in the late 1800s and early 1900s. Most of his activities were in Argentina and Uruguay but from 1879 to 1887 he was Superintendent of Missions in South America, and in this capacity organized missionary work in Paraguay. This collection holds about 25,000 pages of letters and is filed chronologically. A chronological guide is available.

Historical Committee
Archives of the Mennonite Church
1700 South Main Street
Goshen, Indiana 46526

36. Harold S. Bender Collection

This official of the Church was long interested in overseas missions. Box 50 of the Mennonite Central Committee Corresspondence and Institutional Materials through 1938 contains reports of official visits to Paraguay, immigration lists in the 1930s, land purchases and correspondence between Bender and Mennonite settlers. Similar correspondence with colonists is continued in Box 51 through the 1930s and Box 54 through the 1940s. A guide exists.

37. Robert Friedmann

In this collection, under Anabaptist-Mennonite Historical Documents — Later Mennonite and Hutterite Source Materials, Box 45, is a report by Harold S. Bender on a visit to Mennonite Colonies in Paraguay in 1938. A guide exists.

38. Christian L. Graber Collection

Christian L. Graber was a business manager at Goshen College as well as pastor. He had a longtime interest in the Chaco settlements and visited them while working for the Mennonite Central Committee. In Boxes 1 and 7 of this collection are accounts of his visits and observations in the Chaco. A guide exists.

39. Nelson and Ada Litwiller Collection

In Box 3 of this collection are the minutes and reports of the Mission Committee of the Mennonite Church for 1963-1966 that refer to Paraguay, as well as correspondence referring to Church work in the Chaco between 1960 and 1965. A guide exists.

40. Mennonite Central Committee Collection

This collection is the primary archive of the Mennonite Church, and as such is the most important source in the United States of the beginnings of the Mennonite experience in the Paraguayan Chaco. It is broken into various sections, many of which pertain to Paraguay. For instance, IX-2, the Maxwell H. Kratz section contains five boxes of correspondence referring to Russian Relief and Paraguayan immigration from 1920 to 1934. Other sections, such as IX-3-1, the H.S. Bender and Germany section contains four boxes dealing with the passage of Mennonite refugees in 1930 through Germany. One of the most important sections, dealing with the financial arrangements of establishment of the Chaco colonies is IX-3-3, Corporación Paraguaya consisting of fifteen boxes.

This has been an under utilized resource in the study of the Paraguayan Mennonite experience, but analysis of these financial records will undoubtedly shed light upon the reasons for the Mennonite success. And finally, IX-3-5, the John Bender section of some eleven boxes contains the correspondence of a member of the Central Committee who through the 1930s and 1940s paid particular attention to the progress of the Chaco colonies. In other sections of the Central Committee Collection are also useful references to Paraguay. An excellent guide exists to this collection.

41. Elvin V. Snyder Collection

In Box 2 of this collection is an investigation of the new Chaco colonies in 1930 by T. K. Hershey.

42. Walter Quiring Collection

This collection contains, in Boxes 1 and 2, various reports on the politics and conomy of the Mennonite Chaco settlements in the 1930s. A guide exists.

Indiana Historical Society
315 West Ohio Street
Indianapolis, Indiana 46202

43. Carleton McCulloch Papers

McCulloch was an important figure in Hoosier politics during the 1930s and a confident of Meredith Nicholson, envoy to Paraguay. After the latter's posting to Paraguay, he continued to keep in regular contact with McCulloch by mail. These approximately 50 letters, which include mention of diplomatic activities in Asunción, the various battles in the war with Bolivia, a horrific visit to a military hospital, and the 1936 ouster of President Ayala, are all included in the McCulloch Papers.

44. Meredith Nicholson Papers

Nicholson was an Indiana author, journalist, and diplomat. He served as envoy to Paraguay between 1933 and 1934, during the bloodiest phase of the Chaco conflict. His letters to private parties make frequent reference to the war and to the highly militarized environment of Asunción. This collection consists of approximately 12 letters and reports catalogued under Meredith Nicholson Papers, M 221.

Indiana University
Main Library
Bloomington, Indiana 47405

45. Sound Recordings of South American Indian Languages

The Main Library at Indiana University has an outstanding collection of sound recordings of South American Indian languages. Various Guaraní Indian groups of Paraguay received attention. San Pedro. Villa de Rosario. Imaga Indians, 1969 (sound recordings — 19 sound cassettes); Paraguay. Asunción, Guaraní, 1949; and United States, Indiana, Bloomington, Guaraní, 1958 (sound recordings — two sound tape reels).

Other Paraguayan Indian groups represented in the IU collection include the Ache-Guayakí, Mbya, Nivaklé, Makka, Toba, Lengua, and Chiriguano. Among sound recordings dealing with these groups are Paraguay, South American Indians, 1944 (sound recording — six sound reel tapes); Argentina. Gran Chaco region, Ashluslay and Choroti Indians, 1934 (Sound recording — two sound tape reels); Argentina. Buenos Aires, Maca Indians, 1939 (sound recording — 1 sound tape reel).

IOWA

Herbert Hoover Library
West Branch, Iowa 52358

46. Bourke B. Hickenlooper Papers

Senator Hickenlooper, a prominent Republican of the mid-century was greatly interested in Latin America and the relations of the United States with that area of the world. At times in the 1950s and 1960s he chaired the Senate Foreign Relations American Republics Affairs Subcommittee and deposited his papers from that subcommittee in the Hoover Library. There is one folder, Paraguay, that addresses that nation directly. A guide to the Hickenlooper papers exists.

47. Herbert Hoover Papers

In the Presidential Foreign Affairs Series, Countries, portion of the Hoover papers there exists one folder titled, Paraguay 1929-1932, and a folder of endorsements for American diplomats appointed to Asunción. There also is a "Bolivia" folder relative to delegates appointed to the Commission of Inquiry and Conciliation dealing with the Chaco question. The Diplomats File consists of one folder dealing with correspondence with George L. Kreek, Minister to Paraguay in 1929; one folder for Post Wheeler, Minister to Paraguay in 1929-1932; and one of endorsements concerning the appointment of diplomats.

48. Francis White Papers

This prominent diplomat played an important role in the American attempt, through the offices of the Pan American Union, to prevent the Chaco Conflict. In the heading, Chaco, under the sub-file, Conferences and Treaties, there are about 2000 pages of material relating to the Commission of Inquiry and Conciliation, and the Commission of Neutrals. Essentially this material covers the period 1928 to 1933. No one investigating the attitude of the United States toward Paraguay and the Chaco question can afford to neglect this file. In addition, there are several folders within the White Papers containing correspondence with American diplomats over Paraguayan matters. George L. Kreek is represented with one folder containing material from 1927 to 1932; Post Wheeler, a folder covering the years 1930-33; and a general folder simply titled Paraguay, 1929-1933. A finding guide to the White Papers will aid the investigator.

KANSAS

Bethel College
Mennonite Library and Archives
300 East 27th
North Newton, Kansas 67117

49. Board of Missions, Commission on Overseas Missions

In this archive are extensive Mennonite files that pertain to this church's settlement and missionary work in Paraguay. Most important are the Files of the Board of Missions, Commission on Overseas Missions. Box 45, Folders 81-82 deal with Paraguay from 1951-1960; Box 46, Folders Numbers 83-85 deal with various construction projects in the Mennonite colonies in Paraguay. Box 56, Folders 109-111 treat the years 1961-1969, while Box 32 Folder 449 deals with the mission to Paraguay for the years 1970-1979. In the latter box, folders 450-452 are concerned with the Mennonite Asunción Theological Center from 1976 through 1979. Also in Box 32 are folders of the decade of the 1970s that deal with such diverse matters in Paraguay as Indian Work, the Kansas Medical Team dispatched to Paraguay in 1974, Education in the Mennonite Colonies, evangelization, and the papers of Ewald Rein for the years 1975-1977, and those of Jacob Reimer for 1973. A brief guide to the files in this archive is available.

50. Peter C. Hiebert Papers

This archive contains the personal papers of Peter C. Hiebert, active in Mennonite colonization and relief projects in the first half of this century. Box 14, folders 112-122 are particularly relevant to Mennonite colonization in Paraguay in the 1930s. A guide to his papers exists.

51. Abraham M. Lohrentz

The papers of Abraham M. Lohrentz who provided medical service to Mennonites in Paraguay in 1945-1946 are also held by this archive. Box 2 which deals with a medical mission to Paraguay is most relevant. A short guide to the Lohrentz papers also exists.

Dwight D. Eisenhower Library
Abilene, Kansas 67410

52. Dwight D. Eisenhower Papers

Within the Ann Whitman File, the Official File and the General File series of the Eisenhower White House Central Files, and the Records of the White House Staff Secretary are five folders titled, Paraguay. These folders contain correspondence, memoranda, memoranda of conversations, and reports, but much of the material is duplicated and is rather of a routine nature. References to Paraguay are found scattered within those files relating to Export-Import Bank transactions and other foreign economic matters.

The most important material in this presidential library relating to Paraguay is found in the Records of the White House Office of the Special Assistant for National Security Affairs, the National Security Council Staff Papers, the Records of the White House Staff Research Group, and the personal papers of Thomas Mann and Samuel Waugh. The latter two were prominent diplomats during the Eisenhower years and intimately involved in the formulation of policy toward Latin America. Within this material, a researcher will discover the origins of the United States policy toward the Paraguay of General Alfredo Stroessner, and how that policy was governed by Cold War concerns.

Most material is now unclassified, and finding guides exist to aid the researcher at the Eisenhower Library.

University of Kansas
Kenneth Spencer Research Library
Lawrence, Kansas 66045

The state of Kansas has for some time enjoyed a "sister state" relation with the Republic of Paraguay. Perhaps because of this, the University of Kansas Libraries boast some surprisingly rich holdings in Paraguayana.

The great strength of the Kansas holdings can be seen in very impressive documentary collections —most originally assembled by an eminent Paraguayan, Juan Natalicio González (1896-1966). González acted as the chief spokesman for the nationalist wing (Guión Rojo) of the Colorado Party in the post-Chaco War era. He served briefly as president of his country during the late 1940s. He also received wide recognition, even from his political opponents, as one of Paraguay's key intellectuals during the same period. González edited an Asunción literary and historical review, *Guaranía*, which was probably the most influential scholarly journal produced in Paraguay during the 1940s. He also wrote numerous essays on philosophy, sociology, and history. His classical study on Paraguayan national character, *Proceso y formación de la cultura paraguaya* (Asuncion, 1948), even today is still widely read.

The various twists and turns of national politics kept González out of the public eye after he resigned the presidency. When Alfredo Stroessner came to power in a 1954 golpe, however, he appointed González Paraguayan ambassador to Mexico. Almost certainly, General Stroessner thought it advisable to send the always-impressive guionista out of the country rather that permit him to reestablish himself as a possible rival. In any case, González held the ambassador's post for many years.

The Kansas holdings, housed in the Special Collections Department at the Spencer Library, clearly reflect González's many interests, and the collection contains useful material on nearly every phase of Paraguayan history and politics.

53. Actas Capitulares del Calbildo de la Asunción

An extremely valuable source for the colonial era is this seventeen-volume set of transcribed municipal documents from Paraguay's Archivo Nacional and which date from the late 1500s to 1709 (Ms. E206-E220; Ms.G42-G43; Ms. P492:1). Dealing with such topics as Indian-white relations, the governance of the community of Asunción, and the complicated relation that community had with the Jesuit Order, these records would contribute greatly to any study of the little-known, but crucial, seventeenth century. It is worthwhile to note that the originals of some of these actas no longer exist in the Archivo, leaving these copies within the González Collection as perhaps the only ones in existence.

54. Ernesto Alvarado García Collection

This Honduran professor, diplomat, and archivist (born 1904) acted as consul for Paraguay in Tegucigalpa between 1939 and 1941. His papers, which were obtained by the Spencer Library in the 1960s, contain three letters dealing with minor Paraguayan matters.

55. Chaco War Collection

Materials on the more recent history of Paraguay are found in Chaco War (Ms. E199). Maps, order, decrees and reports concerned with military operations (1932-33) are present, many of them with the letterhead "El Estado Mayor" and confidential in nature.

56. Diplomacy Collection

This collection of documents (Ms. E202) springs from the pens of various Paraguayan officials between 1847 and 1914. It consists of about five hundred pages of original manuscripts by such figures as Juan Andrés Gelly, Juan Crisóstomo Centurión, Carmelo and Natalicio Talavera, and Cecilio Báez. As such it is extremely important for any study of Paraguayan diplomatic history in this era.

57. Dr. José Gaspar de Francia. Documents of the Archivo Nacional

The bound set of Dr. José Gaspar de Francia. Documentos del Archivo Nacional de la Asunción (Ms. E194, vols. 1-6) consists of typescript copies of documents (1772-1840) from the various sections of the Archivo, especially the Secciones Historia and Nueva Encuadernación. Volume 1 is titled "Datos biográficos"; volume 2, "El consulado"; and volumes 3-6, "La dictadura." The entire work totals over twenty-five hundred pages, each page stamped "Archivo Nacional." A major advantage of these transcripts over the originals held in Asunción is that the González copies are arranged chronologically and are therefore far easier for the scholar to use.

58. González Personal Collection

Also included in the collection are several personal scrapbooks of González (Mss. E223-224). These contain photographs and original drawings of González, his family and friends; newspaper and manuscript articles about González; calling cards and notes to González in his capacity as dean of the diplomatic corps in Mexico City; and even his school report card for 1908. Also included are two scrapbooks of newspaper clippings and mimeographs on geology, the cultivation of rice and maize in Paraguay, port facilities, transportation, and energy policy for the late 1940s and early 1950s (Mss. E230-231). The collection also features a Spanish-language typescript of Félix de Azara's 1793 *Descripción histórica, physica, política y geográphica del Paraguay* (Ms. E197) —a French edition of this work appeared in 1801, but no Spanish printing has ever been made; also, "Guaraní Indians" (Mss. E195, vols. 1-3, and E196), a four-volume set containing hand and typewritten manuscripts and documents. This item is mainly a Spanish-Guaraní dictionary (400 pages) and grammar (300 pages), although volume four deals with Guaraní botanical terms.

59. Government Reports

The Kansas holdings also include a series of Government Reports (Mss. E225-229), consisting of a January 1926 Dirección General de Estadística report to the Treasury Minister; a 1926 report of the Dirección de Ganadería e Inspector de Carnes; and an August 1935 naval report regarding a "Proyecto de Limpieza del río Paraguay" (includes some curious photographs of buoys and dredges). There is also an interesting 1951 *informe* sent to Minister Tomás Romero Pereira from a special commission for the rehabilitation of the Paraguayan State Railway, and an incomplete 1953 series of the *Boletín Informativo*, issued by the Foreign Affairs Ministry. Bound with the latter is a short printed biography on Dr. Raúl Sapena Pastor. The documentation contained in these various statistical reports might prove of great interest to the quantitative historian.

60. Grupo Staudt Collection

This collection (Ms. E200) consists of one-hundred fifty pages of material, original documents and typewritten copies, relative to the formation, operation, and subsequent government-decreed dissolution of a key economic cartel that operated in Asunción in the late 1940s.

61. Latrocinios Chavistas Collection

This intriguing collection (Ms. E201) contains more than a hundred reports, newspaper accounts, manuscripts and documents on the systematic looting of the National Bank of Paraguay during the Federico Chaves years and up to 1961. Some of the leading families in Paraguay were evidently involved in the thefts.

62. Libros de Real Hacienda

Another long extract from the colonial holdings of the Archivo is a five-volume typed transcription of the Libros de Real Hacienda (Ms.E221). This transcription covers the years 1772 to 1788 and is therefore a prime source for the Intendencia period, especially with regard to the fiscal and commercial structure of the province. Such documentation would be of great importance in understanding the yerba mate trade.

63. Carlos Antonio López. Documents of the Archivo Nacional

A continuation of the Francia volumes is Carlos Antonio López, Documentos del Archivo Nacional (Ms. E193, volumes 1-10). Volume 1 is titled "La familia"; 2, "El consulado"; and 3-10, "La presidencia." Also chronologically arranged, the López compilation consists of some thirty-five hundred pages covering the period 1807 to 1863; each page is again stamped with the official seal of the Archivo. Several copies of portraits of Carlos Antonio López as well as three original manuscript documents signed by López accompany these volumes.

64. Miscellaneous Documents

This collection (Ms. E203) is a four-hundred page set of original documents and manuscripts on the Chaco conflict, national politics in the 1920s and 1930s, and various aspects of literature. This section includes one lengthy typewritten manuscript, "El Dictador Francia," by Marco Antonio Laconich, onetime director of the Archivo Nacional.

65. Victor Morínigo Collection

This collection (Ms. E192, volumes 1 and 2) consists of around six hundred pages and covers Paraguayan diplomacy in the 1930 through 1957 era. Useful sources on the Chaco War and on President Morínigo's role in national politics are here included.

66. Original and Copied Nineteenth Century Material

This collection (Ms. E222) contains some interesting documents from the 1860s, including procesos of criminals and materials detailing the Uruguayana and Corrientes campaigns during the Triple Alliance conflict. Though possibly not as important as the Francia or López archival transcripts, these various letters will interest scholars of the Paraguayan War.

67. Plan of Economic Development

This plan (Ms. E198) is a two-hundred page official government study with additional government reports covering the years 1945 to 1946. It has never been published. Any understanding of Paraguayan economic development in the heady era just before the 1947 civil war could well make use of this document.

68. Río Paraguay Collection

The Kansas Collections are also useful in analyzing the recent economic development of the country. Río Paraguay (Ms. D144) is a complete survey of trade on the Paraguay River between 1917 and 1949. Documents on the history of river commerce, laws, decrees, and geography are included, along with several charts and graphs.

The Actas, Libros de la Real Hacienda, and the Francia and López materials were originally assembled under the direction of Doroteo Bareiro, head of the Archivo in the 1940s. They are all clearly marked as to their location in the Paraguayan archive (though it should be noted that documents marked as being in the SJC — Sección Judicial Criminal — generally have been assigned new *legajo* numbers in Asunción). In the end, it took nearly thirty years after González departed Paraguay for photocopies of the Francia and López compilations to return to the Archivo Nacional thanks to a contribution by North American historian Richard Alan White. Still other photocopies of these same transcripts (though not of those of the Actas or Libros) were made during the 1980s and 1990s and now can be consulted at the libraries of U.C. Riverside, U.C. Los Angeles, and the University of Georgia (in the case of the latter library, only the Francia materials are present). To be sure, however, the Spencer Library holds the original transcripts. The overall value of these materials cannot be overestimated; they represent what is probably the principal source for studies of Paraguayan political and economic structures, diplomatic relations, land tenure, and the history of the military in the era preceding the Triple Alliance War.

KENTUCKY

University of Louisville
William F. Ekstrom Library
Louisville, Kentucky 40292

69. Archivo Nacional de Asunción

The University of Louisville possesses on microfilm acquired from the Instituto Panamericano de Geografía e Historia volumes of the Sección Histórica of the Archivo Nacional de Asunción for the years approximately 1750-1850. Until recently this was the only catalogued section (and crudely at that) of the Asunción archive and in the Sección Histórica are found cabildo records, orders of viceroys, daily business of governors, relations with Indians — the entire gamut of colonial government records. It is also indispensable for a study of the Independence Era, the regime of Dr. José Gaspar de Francia, and the epoch of the two López. An idea of the variety of documents within a volume can be gained by referring to a single number:

> Archivo Nacional de Asunción, Sección Histórica, volume 198-Año 1805. Expediente acerca de unos portugueses llegados al Paraguay. Contrabando de tabaco. Reglamento para los carniceros. Reparación de la casa del govierno en ruinas. Remate de diezmos. Comprobación de pesas y medidas en Ñeembucú. Quejas contra el teniente asesor. Falta de caudales en la tesorería. Guarda del almacén real. Extracción y compra clandestina de tabaco. Publicación de una orden del gobernador en Curuguaty. Correspondencia de Asunción y del gobernador (borrador).

This microfilm is held by multi-media of the Ekstrom Library and is available on interlibrary loan. Borrowers should identify their needs by volume number from Francisco Sevillano Colóm, "Lista del contendio de los volúmenes microfilmados del Archivo Nacional de Asunción," *Hispanic American Historical Review*, 38:1 (February, 1958), pp. 60-120.

In addition, the Patterson Rare Book Collection of Ekstrom Library possesses a typescript "Archivo Nacional Libro No. 6, 7, 9, 14 Año 1803 1805 18ll Libro Mayor de la Real Caxa del Paraguay del Cargo de los Minist. Paraguay Archivo Nacional." These are the fiscal records of the Intendencia del Paraguay (Cajas Reales) from 1803 to 1811. Obviously they were copied by someone well acquainted with the Intendencia treasury records.

MAINE

Maine Historical Society
485 Congress Street
Portland, Maine 04101

70. John S. H. Fogg Collection

In the John S. H. Fogg Collection, Volume 43, there is a letter dated Asunción, December 28, 1845, from President Carlos Antonio López of Paraguay to ? (illegible). This letter, obviously translated from the Spanish, deals with the mission of Edward A. Hopkins and international affairs in the Platine region. It is useful for anyone studying the origin of relations between the United States and Paraguay.

MARYLAND

Agricultural Department
National Agricultural Library
Main Library
10301 Baltimore Boulevard
Beltsville, Maryland 20705

71. National Agricultural Library

The strength of this library is its worldwide collection of bound volumes pertaining to agriculture and all related subjects. There are, however, various primary sources such as reports and statistical coverage on such varied matters as land usage, rural education, and agricultural and pastoral law. National and international commissions' reports are also found here. Paraguay is well represented and for an analysis of that vitally important economic sector for that republic, this library should not be neglected. It is open to the public and has a multitude of published catalogs, card collections, bibliographies, and on-line data bases to aid the investigator. One should get in touch with the library to facilitate bibliographic search procedures.

National Archives at College Park
8601 Adelphi Road
Presidential Materials Project
College Park, Maryland 20740

72. Richard M. Nixon Papers

Most of the presidential papers of Richard M. Nixon are yet in the hands of the National Archives. Within these materials of the Presidential Materials Project are the White House Central Files (Subject Files) relating to South America from 1969 through 1973 in Boxes 8 and 9, Country File 1-9. Sporadic mention of Paraguay may be found in them. In Box 60 of this segment are the specific Paraguay Files, Country File 118, covering the years 1969-1971. A guide exists. Another part of these materials, the White Central Files (Subject Files — Foreign Affairs), contains scattered mention of Paraguay but no files directly pertaining to that nation. A guide exists to general topics and any investigator must begin there. The same holds true for the White House Central Files (Subject Files — International Organizations,) and White House Central Files — Department of State). Some restrictions yet apply on the use of Nixon materials.

National Institutes of Health
National Library of Medicine
Public Health Service
Department of Health and Human Services
8600 Rockville Pike
Bethesda, Maryland 20894

73. Fred Soper Papers

The National Library of Medicine holds the Papers of Fred Soper who worked in Paraguay for the International Health Division of the Rockefeller Foundation in the early and mid-1920s. There he was engaged in the campaign against hookworm. Items that specifically refer to Paraguay are his diaries for the 1920s, found in containers 6 and 7, unpublished papers found in container 23, and notes on yellow fever in Paraguay in container 37. These papers (Call Number: MS C 359) are open to qualified researchers and a finding guide is available in the library. (Also see the entry on the Rockefeller Foundation.)

Archives of the General Conference of the Seventh-Day Adventists
12501 Old Columbia Pike
Silver Spring, Maryland 20904

74. Seventh-Day Adventists

This archive houses the records covering the entire history of this church. The missionary activities of the Seventh-Day Adventists in Paraguay are found in the minutes of the Record Group of the South American Division, as well as in the general correspondence files of other record groups. There exists a general guide to this archive and interested scholars should first get in touch with the staff of this institution. The archive is open to researchers but some restrictions apply on certain materials.

MASSACHUSETTS

Boston Public Library
Copley Square
Boston, Massachusetts 02117

75. Boston Public Library Manuscript Collection

In addition to a very good general collection of Paraguayan published works, the Boston Public Library has one original document of interest to those scholars researching the Triple Alliance War: Autographed letter of Lt. Commander W. A. Kirkland of the U.S.S. *Wasp* to Rear Admiral Charles Henry Davis, Montevideo, 22 Sept. 1868, in which Kirkland reports result of his mission to Paraguay and refers to his various meetings with Francisco Solano López — 13 sheets. 13 pp. (ms. 2604).

John Fitzgerald Kennedy Library
Columbia Point
Boston, Massachusetts 02125

76. John Fitzgerald Kennedy Papers

Within this presidential library there are scattered materials relating to Paraguay within the National Security Files, the President's Office Files, and the White House Central Files. The National Security Files are essentially the foreign policy file of the Kennedy White House. The White House Central Files are well cataloged. Often restrictions apply to the use of these files so a researcher is advised to ascertain their availability in advance.

Harvard University
Widener Library
Cambridge, Massachusetts 02138

77. Documents Collection

Within this collection are a few extremely interesting documents from various periods of Paraguayan history ranging from the Treaty of Madrid in 1750 the War of the Triple Alliance (1864-1870). A guide exists.

78. Pamphlet Collection

The Widener Library possesses an impressive collection of pamphlet boxes, of which there are some twenty-seven. These boxes hold published materials not otherwise catalogued in the Harvard indexes. Since so much of Paraguayan history and politics has only been recorded in pamphlet form, these boxes represent a possible treasure trove for the assiduous researcher. Of course, each box varies greatly as to quality of materials contained therein. The topics covered in the pamphlet boxes include the Paraguayan constitution, the army, the Triple Alliance War, the López "Tyranny," Statistics, Economic Resources, Church history, Emigration, Asunción, Periodicals, Freemasons, Crime, Boundaries with Bolivia, Education, and the Tariff.

79. Theodore Roosevelt Papers

Harvard also has 500 linear feet of documents associated with President Theodore Roosevelt (1858-1919); some of the letters that Roosevelt wrote from Paraguay during his mid-1910's hunting and exploration visit to that country are contained in this collection.

80. University Students.

Harvard possesses a survey of 482 Paraguayan university students, carried out by S. M. Lipset in 1966. Their values, vocational, and political orientations were analyzed. Researchers have unrestricted use of this data.

MICHIGAN

Gerald R. Ford Library
1000 Beal Avenue
Ann Arbor, Michigan 48109

81. Gerald Ford Papers

In the White House Central Files, under Subject Files, Box 41, Country 118-Paraguay there are a few items of routine diplomatic correspondence. One interesting topic is the correspondence surrounding the flight of the Paraguayan Ambassador, Miguel Solano López, to Asunción in 1976 so that that diplomat might die in his native homeland. Researchers should be aware that the most substantive collections on foreign affairs, the files of Henry Kissinger and Brent Scowcroft, are not yet processed and therefore not available to research at the present time.

MINNESOTA

St. Olaf College
Norwegian-American Historical Association Archives
Northfield, Minnesota 55057

82. Nicolay Andrew Grevstad Papers.

Nicolay Andrew Grevstad was a Minnesota newspaperman and politician. He served as United States Minister to Paraguay and Uruguay in 1911-1914. Among his papers relating to Paraguay are despatches to the United States State Department, press releases, material on investment opportunities, and general correspondence. Open to qualified researchers with certain restrictions.

MISSISSIPPI

University of Southern Mississippi
William David McCain Library and Archives
Hattiesburg, Mississippi 39406

83. International Archives of Latin American Political Posters

The International Archives of Latin American Political Posters houses one of the world's largest collections of posters from Latin America. It contains in excess of 10,000 posters, mostly produced by political parties, labor unions, exile groups, and government agencies. Only forty-two of this large number come from Paraguay, and all of these focus on the Stroessner and post-Stroessner periods. The earliest poster — a portrait sketch of the general — dates from 1955. The latest posters are all drawn from the much-contested 1991 election. The Paraguay holdings do not include any tourism oriented posters.

MISSOURI

Saint Louis University
Knights of Columbus Vatican Film Library
221 North Grand
Saint Louis, Missouri 63103

This microfilm library possesses some of the finest sources on the Jesuit experience in the New World, and as such, are quite important for anyone dealing with this order's works in the Río de Plata, and especially the Paraguayan missions. The holdings are in various collections.

84. Archivum Romanum Societatis Iesu

This archive is the official depository of the Society and St. Louis University has extensive microfilm holdings of it. It is strong for the pre-expulsion order in Spanish America, and most of its documentation never appeared in Latin American archives. There is a basic finding guide to this collection, but the researcher is warned that there are extensive gaps in the records as war, plague, persecution and other vicissitudes took their toll. Nonetheless, it has much to interest historians of the Paraguayan Jesuit Missions. For the pre-expulsion order, there are three primary groupings; the first by geographical jurisdictions of the order; the second in which materials bearing on the order as a whole are filed; and the third *Libri Impressi*. Various sub-groupings within these three groups aid the researcher to relevant material.

85. Fondo Gesuitico al Gesu

This Fondo is basically the Procurator General's archive. In the "old" order the Procurator General was both treasurer of the Society and the chief liaison officer with various papal congregations. For Paraguayan studies the mass of material that accumulated in his office because he was treasurer has great value. This collection holds the letters from individual Jesuits who requested mission assignments. The economic documents make it possible to trace the material story of many Jesuit enterprises, not least among them the missions of Paraguay. There are inventories for much of the Fondo material but no calendar.

86. P. Pablo Pastells Collection — Serie Primera

This collection comprises documents transcribed from the Archivo de Indias in Sevilla, Spain and then microfilmed. It is made up of 126 volumes of documents that the Jesuit researcher P. Pablo Pastells assembled from the Secretaría del Perú (57 volumes), and from the Secretaría de Nueva España (69 volumes). Within each viceroyalty division the materials are grouped by audiencia — Lima, Charcas, etc. Each volume contains about 600 folios, most transcribed by hand, although many were copied by typewriter during the later years of the project. Each volume is preceded by a calendar-index of its documents. Care was taken that copies reflect exactly the originals. The documents themselves are communications by royal officials in the Indies and Jesuit superiors to the crown, royal orders and communications by the Crown, all types of requests and reports on missions, as well as polemics reflecting the long-standing conflicts between Jesuits and officials, or Jesuits and other orders. It is essential for a study of this order's missions in Paraguay.

Missouri Historical Society
225 South Skinker
Saint Louis, Missouri 63105

---

87. Daily Morning Herald

The Saint Louis *Daily Morning Herald* was an important local newspaper in the Midwest during the mid-nineteenth century. In October and November 1858 the paper published a series of letters from James F. Milligan, then a lieutenant in the U.S. Navy stationed at Norfolk, Virginia. In these letters Milligan made broad comment on the naval expedition then being prepared to send against Paraguay as a response to the *Water Witch* incident of several years earlier. Milligan made some incisive (and rather disparaging) remarks on Commodore William Shubrick's political moves to gain the senior position in the South Atlantic fleet. Unfortunately, holdings of the *Daily Morning Herald* are now extremely rare, and the only existing copies for 1858 can be found at the Missouri Historical Society in Saint Louis. Those researchers interested in U.S.-Paraguay relations and wishing to consult the Milligan letters should refer to the Society's newspaper collection.

Harry S. Truman Library
U.S. Highway 24 and Delaware Street
Independence, Missouri 64050

---

88. Harry S. Truman Papers

Official File 338 of the Truman library contains several manuscript collections of interest to Paraguayanists. One is a letter of 74 pages concerning trade relations between the United States and Paraguay during the Truman years. Other correspondence in this file mainly concerns endorsements for ambassadorships to Paraguay, gifts to the President, greetings, congratulations, etc. Official File 306 contains documents (10 pages) concerning Fletcher Warren, an Ambassador to Paraguay appointed by President Truman. Official File 1435 contains 5 pages of documents relative to the appointment of George P. Shaw to be Ambassador to Paraguay. And Official File 2945 holds 13 pages relative to the appointment of Howard H. Tewksbury to be Ambassador to Asunción.

The President's Secretary's File (PSF) contains documents on Paraguay in the President's Appointments File (4 pages) relating to a meeting on April 23, 1948. The PSF also contains Central Intelligence Agency Reports in which Paraguay is mentioned — ORE 16/1 and ORE 22-49, of about five pages.

Under the subject portion "P" of the Foreign Affairs File, there is correspondence among President Truman, Ambassador to Paraguay Fletcher Warren, and State Department Official James Bruce, all concerned with United States relations with Paraguay in the mid-1940s.

All the above files in the Truman Library are open to researchers.

University of Missouri at Columbia
Western Historical Manuscript Collection
23 Ellis Library
Columbia, Missouri 65201

89. Board of Foreign Scholarships

Folders 3168,3251, 3276, and 3310 of collection 2582 are the Paraguayan Annual Reports to the Board of Foreign Scholarships of the United States State Department for the years 1956-1960. Included are evaluations of the lecturers, students, and research scholars in Paraguay under Fulbright auspices. Individuals are filed alphabetically within the year reported.

90. Sara Lockwood Williams Papers

Collection 2533, folder 1204 are the papers and travel accounts of a journalist, Sara Lockwood Williams (1885-1961), pertaining to Paraguay.

NEW JERSEY

Princeton University
Harvey Firestone Library
Princeton, New Jersey 08544

91. Princeton University Latin American Pamphlet Collection

Within this collection is an interesting set of pamphlets, papers, journal articles, speeches, legal documents, etc., relating to the "Constitutions of Paraguay, 1963-1987." Each title in the collection has been catalogued with bibliographic access on line by means of RLIN and OCLC. One may order the entire Paraguayan set on microfilm. The "Constitutions of Paraguay" will greatly aid any scholar working on the Stroessner years in that republic and the manipulation of the constitutional process.

NEW YORK

United Nations
Dag Hammarskjold Library
United Nations Plaza
New York, New York 10017

92. Dag Hammarskjold Library

The Hammarskjold Library is the official repository of the United Nations. As such, it possesses all the documents generated by this body. More than that, however, it received in the early 1950s the Woodrow Wilson Memorial Library concentrating on the League of Nations and also receives pertinent copies of documentary material generated by other specialized world bodies such as the World Health Organization, the International Labor Organization, UNESCO, etc. In addition, it receives the white papers, official gazettes, ministerial decrees, statistical collections, and many other publications of all nations in the world.

From the beginning this library was designed to serve the needs of the United Nations staff and representatives of member states so it by no means can be considered a general library. Indeed, its collection of monographs is rather meager when measured against the vast number of documents it possesses. For the latter reason, it is of special interest to anyone investigating the role of Paraguay in this world body, as well as that nation's participation in the various scientific and cultural activities in other world agencies.

The documentation from the League of Nations will interest those investigating the origins of the Chaco War, and the diplomacy surrounding that conflict. Other, more recent documentation deals with such varied matters as freedom of the press, human rights, genocide, and narcotics, all issues of importance in Paraguay since the 1960s.

The library has special interests in economics, international law, international relations, and more recently, environmental issues. Monthly it issues the *Current Bibliographical Information*, and irregularly the *United Nations Documents Index*, and various indices to the proceedings of the General Assembly, Economic and Social Council, the Security Council, and the Trustee Council, as well as subject bibliographies.

The library is generally restricted to the staff of missions to the United Nations and to the Secretariat staff. Non-attached, qualified users are admitted upon special request. This general restriction is not as onerous as one might suppose since leading American libraries act as United Nations Depository Libraries for documentary material. They receive the complete mimeographed documents of the United Nations, as well as receiving, upon subscription, the complete printed documentation of that body. Such libraries have the full gamut of guides, bibliographies, etc., and their regional locations facilitate the researcher's task. This is a source for the study of modern Paraguay that has been very underutilized.

Hispanic Society of America Library
613 West 155th Street
New York, New York 10032

93. William Stewart Collection

An important holding by the Hispanic Society is a two volume compilation of sixty-five memorials, evidences, issues, records, and other papers referring to the "Cause of William Stewart M.D., late of Paraguay, now in Edinburgh, pursuer, and Antoine Gelot, in Paris, defender, treated at Edinburgh from 1870 to 1878." This compilation, evidently copied from originals in the Scottish Records Office, is full of rarely-seen testimony from many luminaries of the Francisco Solano López period, including Madame Lynch and Juan Crisóstomo Centurión.

New York Public Library
Fifth Avenue and 47th Street
New York, New York 10018

94. John Jay Almy Papers

John Jay Almy (1815-1895), was a U.S. naval officer whose long career included participation in the Paraguay expedition of 1858-1859.

95. Walter B. Graham Papers

The documents section also contains the papers of Walter B. Graham (b. 1878), secretary to a U.S. Minister to Paraguay at the beginning of the century.

96. Obadiah Rich Collection

The NYPL's Obadiah Rich collection of colonial Latin American documents contains some rare and very useful items of interest to the Paraguayanist. Two major historical periods predominate: (A) The conquest and early exploration of Paraguay in the mid-1500s, especially the Ayolas, Martínez de Irala, and Cabeza de Vaca episodes; and (B) The anti-Jesuit campaigns of Fray Bernardino de Cárdenas, the Bishop of Asunción some hundred years later. In the latter case, the documents are mostly made up of handwritten transcripts, evidently made in 1780, of letters originally penned in the 1600s. The Paraguayan materials as a whole are stored in Folios 6 and 25. Guides exist. Some examples of these documents are:

1. 246r-247r   Gabriel de Peralta, dean of the Asunción cathedral to the president of the Council of the Indies, regarding cruelty to the Indians (Asunción, 18 May 1653).

2. 248r   Anon., "Cargos que se hacen a los padres de la Compañia de Jesús en el Paraguay" (c.1663).

3. 252r-254v   Bishop Bernardino de Cárdenas to Padre Melchor Maldonado, bishop of Tucumán, re jurisdiction over the missions (Corrientes, 3 Jan. 1645).

4. 44r-53v   Francisco Villalta to [Council of the Indies?], re expeditions of Juan de Ayolas and Alvar Núñez Cabeza de Vaca (Asunción, 22 June 1556).

5. 54r-59r   Martín González to Council of the Indies], re power struggles within the province (Asunción, 25 Apr. 1546).

6. 60r-65r   Francisco Ortíz de Vergara, re his arrival and conflict with Domingo Martínez de Irala, and expeditions (into Chaco?) (np, post-1540).

7. 83r-100r   Pedro Fernández to Emperor Charles V, re the arrival of Pedro de Mendoza and, later, of Alvar Núñez

Cabeza de Vaca, the expeditions of Juan Ayolas, and the revolt of Domingo Martínez de Irala (Asunción, 28 Jan. 1545).

Rockefeller Archive Center
15 Dayton Avenue
North Tarrytown, New York 10591

97. Rockefeller Foundation

In this archive are various records relating to Rockefeller Foundation projects in Paraguay, most touching on matters of public health and education. In Record Group 1.1 Projects, Series 329 Paraguay (1919-1942), Box Number One contains various folders relating to the control of hookworm in the 1920s, and the control of yellow fever in the 1930s and 1940s, as well as general correspondence concerning public health in Paraguay. An interesting report, "Medical Education and Public Health in Paraguay," composed by North American medical specialists in Paraguay during the years 1919-1925 may be found in folder three of this box. Box Number Two contains several folders relating to visits to the universities of Asunción in 1960 and various agricultural visits to Paraguay in the years 1968-1969.

Record Group 2 holds the general correspondence of the Rockefeller Foundation for the years 1927-1951. Under series 239 Paraguay (a section of the Individual Nation Files), Box Number Nine is administrative correspondence. The communications of Dr. Fred Soper (see Library of Medicine holdings also) for 1929 are in Box Number Twenty-five, folder 204. Other boxes contain yearly Paraguayan correspondence and the location of such papers may be ascertained quite easily from the finding guide of the archive.

Record Group 5 - International Health Board/Division, Series 1.2 Correspondence, Project, contains material on Paraguay for the early part of the twentieth century. In this record group are some important reports on the control of hookworm in Paraguay and the state of public health in that nation. Series 2 , Box Number Thirty-five in this group contains some interesting reports on these matters.

The Rockefeller Archive Center has important material upon education, public health, and rural life in Paraguay in the first forty years of this century. Yet it rarely has been utilized, even by scholars specializing in those topics. This archive is open to qualified scholars. Excellent finding guides exist, and collections are described in RLIN.

Franklin D. Roosevelt Library
259 Albany Post Road
Hyde Park, New York 12538

98. Franklin D. Roosevelt Papers

Within the President's Official File (OF 338) there is one file titled "Paraguay" and
another on the Chaco dispute (OF 338C). The President's Secretary's File (PSF) also
has a file on Paraguay. Indices are somewhat incomplete but there are references
to Paraguay in the Official File under the State Department (OF 20), and in the
President's Secretary's Files under the State Department, Argentina, and Peru. Cross
references in these files mention Paraguay in more than thirty other files. One
example is found in the United States Tariff Commission File (OF 60) in which Dr.
Harold D. Gresham was assigned to assist the Paraguayan government in the
modernization of its customs administration.

The President's Personal Papers holds files for General José Estigarribia (PPF 6317),
and General Higínio Morínigo (PPF 6417). In these same papers are references to
Paraguay in Latin American Republics (PPF 150). The Harry Hopkins Papers include
Federal Bureau of Investigation reports on Axis activities in Latin America, including
Paraguay, while the Map Room Papers include military and warfare files on South
America, as well as O.S.S. bulletins. The records of the War Refugee Board contains
documents dealing with cooperation with Latin American governments, including
Paraguay.

For the formulation of policy toward Paraguay before and during World War II, one
should investigate the files on the Inter-American Conferences on American
Republics (OF 1970), the Ministers of Foreign Affairs of the American Republics (OF
4074), that of the Coordinator of Inter-American Affairs (OF 4512), and Pan-
American Affairs (OF 87). References to Paraguay are found in all. Guides to all
these parts of the FDR Papers exist.

United Nations
United Nations Centre for Science and Technology for Development
One United Nations Plaza
Rm DC1-1070
New York, New York 10017

99. United Nations Centre for Science and Technology for Development

This center serves the United Nations community and specializes in questions of energy, development, and the environment. Most of its documentary holdings are UN generated. Among them will be primary material relating to Paraguay and hydro-electric power, rural development, and the protection of the environment. This center has its own cataloguing and publishes *UPDATE*, a quarterly devoted to acquisitions.

NORTH CAROLINA

Duke University
William R. Perkins Library
Durham, North Carolina 27708

100. Louis M. Goldsborough Papers

Goldsborough (1805-1877) was a U.S. naval officer who visited Paraguay in 1860. While in Asunción, he sent a short series of letters to his family describing his experiences and these letters now make up part of the Duke collection. Goldsborough later went on to become superintendent of the U.S. Naval Academy.

101. John MacIntosh Kell Papers

Included are some notes discussing President Carlos Antonio López (1858).

102. The Benjamin Muse Papers

These papers (1933) have some minor references to Paraguay in this U.S. diplomat's letters from South America.

103. The Socialist Party of America Papers

These include a minor collection of newspaper clippings on the Chaco War (1932-1935).

104. The Charles Steedman Papers

Steedman was a rear admiral in the U.S. Navy who participated as a young officer in the Paraguay expedition of 1858-1859. Included here is a February 1859 letter that refers to the amicable settlement of the recent dispute between Paraguay and the United States.

OHIO

Rutherford B. Hayes Presidential Center
Spiegel Grove
Fremont, Ohio 43420

105. William Maxwell Evarts Papers

Present at the Hayes Center are the William Maxwell Evarts Papers for 1872-1883. Evarts was Secretary of State at the time of the Hayes Award. This collection of papers is made up of original correspondence, rather than microfilm. It is unclear, however, whether anything here addresses the arbitration question because the collection has only an alphabetical rather than a subject index.

106. Rutherford B. Hayes Papers

Although usually considered a minor president in the United States, Rutherford B. Hayes enjoys considerable fame in Paraguay. This is due to the American president's role in the Chaco Arbitration of 1878 in which the Ohioan settled a land dispute between Argentina and Paraguay in favor of the latter. The Paraguayans, ecstatic that they could win this decision after having lost so much only ten years earlier in the Triple Alliance War, gratefully named this section of the Chaco in honor of Hayes.

The Hayes Presidential Center in Fremont, Ohio, houses the presidential library with 75,000 volumes and over 3,100 linear feet of manuscript and photographic material appertaining to the Hayes administration and to Ohio history. Nonetheless, only a tiny portion of this mass of material addresses Paraguay.

The Center has on hand a large bank of vertical files with folders on various research subjects. One of these files concerns Paraguay. Within it one can encounter thirty-six sheets of correspondence, periodical articles, and miscellaneous notes. There is some information here on the 1956 negotiations to obtain a bronze bust of Hayes (it presently graces the entryway to the Hayes primary school in Villa Hayes).

In addition to the Paraguay file, the Center has microfilm copies of all of the president's official correspondence (some 35 rolls of incoming correspondence for 1877-1879 and another two of outgoing correspondence). No subject index exists for these microfilm holdings.

Finally, the Hayes Center has a small holding of printed works on Paraguay and four letters, typed copies in the main, dealing with Paraguay's boundary dispute with Argentina in the late 1870s.

Miami University
King Library
Oxford, Ohio 45056

107. Robert Cumming Schenck Papers

Miami University possesses the papers of Robert Cumming Schenck, United States Minister to the Empire of Brazil from 1851-1853. In this period, he was involved in helping to negotiate a treaty between Brazil and Paraguay. There are a few minor papers touching upon that negotiation. A finding aid is available for this collection.

Oberlin College
Oberlin College Archive
420 Mudd Center
148 West College Street
Oberlin, Ohio 44074

108. Wesley Frost Papers

Within the archives of Oberlin College are the papers of Wesley Frost (1884-1968). Frost was an alumnus of this college and a professional diplomat. Among his various foreign services, he was United States Minister to Paraguay in 1940 and 1941, and then appointed Ambassador to the same republic in 1942. He retired from the post as Senior Career Ambassador in 1944. The papers held by Oberlin document his diplomatic career as well as his personal life. For the Paraguayan service there are file copies of official communications between Frost and Secretary of State Cordell Hull in Series II, Subseries 1 & 2, Box 2. In the collection are also other papers of a more personal nature but still referring to his work in Asunción. The Accession Number for this collection is 75, and the call number OCA 30/30. A guide to Frost's life and career, as well as to the collection is available from the archive. This collection should prove useful for anyone interested in the relations of the United States and Paraguay during World War II.

OREGON

University of Oregon
Knight LIbrary
Eugene, Oregon 97403

109. Hazel Chamberlain Papers

Chamberlain was a U.S.-born missionary teacher in Villarrica and Concepción between 1922 and 1925. Working for the Inland South American Missionary Union of New York, she sent many missives of an official and personal nature back to the United States during this time. Forty-six such items are present in the Oregon collection, including photos of mission personnel and buildings.

RHODE ISLAND

Rhode Island Historical Society
110 Benevolent Street
Providence, Rhode Island 02906

110. United States and Paraguay Navigation Company Papers

The Rhode Island Historical Society possesses the records of the United States and Paraguay Navigation Company, 1852-1891. Edward A. Hopkins, United States Consul in Asunción in the 1850s, was associated with this firm, and in that decade his activities were a focus of controversy between the government of Carlos Antonio López and that of the United States. There are about three feet of records, among which are correspondence, minutes of annual, directors', and special meetings, financial records, company registers, and consular registers of Hopkins for the years 1853-1855. At the Paraguayan end are also business records kept by Hopkins. Much of the correspondence and reports deal with the Paraguayan government's confiscation of the company's property in that republic in the mid-1850s, an action that had its repercussion in the *Water Witch* episode of the same decade. This collection is of prime interest to anyone interested in the early relations of Paraguay with the United States. There is a short historical note and inventory of the collection available from the depository. The call number of this collection is U54spnc.

TENNESSEE

The Historical Commission of the Southern Baptist Convention
Southern Baptist Historical Library and Archives
Suite 400
901 Commerce Street
Nashville, Tennessee 37203

111. The Southern Baptist Historical Library and Archives

In this archive are over 600 feet of records of the Foreign Mission Board of the Southern Baptist Convention. Some relate to mission activities in Paraguay. Within the collection AR.551.1 is the pertinent material on Baptist work in Paraguay. In Boxes 30 and 31 are minutes of the Foreign Mission Board relating to activities in that country for the years 1955 through 1967, as well as annual reports on missionary work there from 1959 to 1976. In Box 4178 are Annual Reports from 1977 to 1987 as well as other material dealing with evangelism and church development, and particularly information upon the Baptist Hospital in Asuncion from the 1950s through the 1970s. Box 4179 also contains much information upon the hospital in the same period as well as other community health and nutrition projects. Mission minutes for the 1980s are also in Box 4179.

There is a guide to these records. Bibliographic database searches are available through OCLU and EPIC. However, access to mission minutes requires permission of the Foreign Mission Board.

TEXAS

University of Texas at Austin
Nettie Lee Benson Library
Austin, Texas 78712

---

112. Archivo Nacional de Asunción

On permanent loan from Miami University of Oxford, Ohio, are microfilm copies of selected volumes of the Sección Histórica of the Archivo Nacional de Asunción. These volumes are 245, 249-251, 255, 261-267, 272, 280-281, 288, 291, 302-307, 312, 316, and 319-356. These volumes are extremely strong for the 1850s and 1860s, and, as such, they complement the similar holdings at the University of Louisville.

113. Manuel E. Gondra Manuscript Collection

The best known and best catalogued of all the Paraguayan materials at the University of Texas is the Manuel Gondra Collection. Gondra (1871-1927) was one of the most-respected scholars of his generation. He had wide-ranging interests in literature, linguistics, and national history, and at the turn of the century published many essays in all of these fields. His political advancement was rapid. In ten years he rose from educator and writer to president of the republic, having served in the interim as Minister of Education, envoy plenipotentiary to Brazil, and Paraguayan delegate to the Third Interamerican Conference of 1906.

The deeper that Gondra moved into politics the further he removed himself from the world of scholarship. The decision to take this route ultimately was an unhappy one for Gondra in that he constantly found himself the victim of circumstance and intrigue. Although he was president on three different occasions, he served a total of less than two years as chief executive. In his last administration (1920-1921) he was falsely accused of tampering with government funds and he left office feeling deeply despondent. He found solace in study, and more particularly, in amassing a huge collection of books, pamphlets, and documents on Paraguayan themes. He was interested, for example, in locating materials that might shed light on the Paraguay-Bolivia land dispute over the Gran Chaco region. He had his agents copy hundreds of documents from European archives and tracked down other documents on the Chaco in Paraguay itself. More and more, the compiling of new materials for his collection became his primary interest. By the time of his death in 1927 Asunceños widely regarded him as a scholarly recluse, more interested in his books and index files than in contemporary national politics.

Gondra's death was followed shortly thereafter by the Great Depression and, with it, some considerable financial pressures on his heirs. Reluctantly, in the summer of 1939, they sold to the University of Texas at Austin the entire Gondra Collection of 7,283 printed books, 2,633 pamphlets, 270 maps, and over 20,000 pages of manuscript sources.

Thirteen years later Carlos Eduardo Castañeda and Jack Autrey Dabbs published an admirable *Calendar of the Manuel E. Gondra Manuscript Collection* (Mexico, 1952). This is still the standard guide to the collection. It lists the documents (and maps) in chronological order (dividing them into sixteenth, seventeenth, eighteenth, nineteenth, and twentieth-century categories), giving author, place, and a short description, and the original archive or source from which the manuscript was transcribed. The *Calendar* also provides an excellent index and several helpful reference lists.

The variety of documents in the Gondra Collection is so rich that the *Calendar* must be consulted in order to appreciate them. To sample their varied nature and to indicate their potential value, however, we will list some of the holdings for the year 1748:

> 1063. Consejo de Indias? [Carta a José Manzo agradeciendo las derrotas infligidas a los indios bárbaros de Tucumán y avisando del nombramiento de Juan Vitorino Martínez de Tineo para la gobernación de dicha provincia]. Madrid, April 13, 1748. 2 l. 17 x 23 cm. f. 1-2. Modern copy from AGI 124-1-10-B [MG 70 1709a]. Mentions letter of Alonso Espinosa de los Monteros describing campaigns against Mocovís y Guaicurús.

> 1066. Larrazábal, Marcos José de. [Carta al Marqués de la Ensenada en que solicita levantamiento de impuestos y de la

obligación de pasar por Santa Fe a los productos del Paraguay] Asunción, June 25, 1748. 3 l. 17 x 23 cm. Modern copy from AGI 124-1-10-A. [MG 1711].

1067. Andonaegui, José de. [Carta al Marqués de la Ensenada comunicándole algunos datos sobre la sangrienta guerra sostenida por los indios del Chaco y el subsiguiente establecimiento de dos pueblos por los padres de la Compañía de Jesús.] Buenos Aires, July 23, 1748. 3 l. 17 x 23 cm. f. 2-4. Modern copy from AGI 124-1-12-C. [MG 1063b]. Attacks on provinces of Paraguay and Tucumán.

The great majority of the documents described in the *Calendar of the Gondra Collection*, especially those dealing with the colonial era, are modern copies from European archives. A good many of the nineteenth and twentieth-century documents, however, are originals, and there are some unusual items among their number: an 1801 report from the Marqués de Avilés to Viceroy Joaquín del Pino outlining social, economic, and political conditions in the Misiones and Paraguay [MG 2056]; an 1812 note to the Paraguayan Junta gubernativa from an official in Concepción discussing negotiations with the Portuguese governor of Coimbra over an exchange of Indian prisoners [MG 1931b]; an 1861(?) essay on "la fraternidad y la unión" probably authored by journalist Natalicio Talavera [MG 1970j]; a series of 48 letters (1862-65) from Paraguayan agent Juan José Soto, then stationed in Montevideo, to various individuals in Uruguay and Argentina, detailing political and commercial affairs in the Río de la Plata [MG 2010a-2010av]; an 1868 Paraguayan troop roster (for the 2nd company, 4th squadron of the 32nd regiment) written on rawhide [MG 2003]; and a 1902 letter from Angel Battilana to the Interior Minister regarding Guido Boggiani's stay in the Gran Chaco [MG 1985].

As noted in the *Calendar*, the map section of the Gondra Collection is exceedingly interesting. It contains maps and charts from the eighteenth through the twentieth century, most of them available nowhere else. Gondra's special interest in the Chaco question is evident here throughout. For example, one blueprint map [index no. 2836] shows various sites along the Río Pilcomayo in 1906. Perhaps the most curious maps of all, however, appear in the *Calendar* as index no. 2824: twenty-two separate hand-drawn maps of Paraguay, the various U.S. states, Cuba, Brazil, Mexico, Central America, Peru, and the West Indies, all produced by the students of Asunción's Instituto de Filosofía in 1857 and dedicated to President Carlos Antonio López (these young students included among their number several individuals of later consequence including memorialist Juan Crisóstomo Centurión and journalist Natalicio Talavera).

Castañeda and Dabbs organized the *Calendar* in such a way so as to enable the researcher to determine whether he or she should come to Austin to examine a given manuscript personally. This goal was very nearly achieved. Nonetheless, the *Calendar* does contain a few mistakes of substance (not surprising in a compilation of thousands of documents). Some errors are minor: the Paraguayan surname "Matiauda" is invariably rendered "Matianda." Still, in a few instances, the entry descriptions are simply inadequate. The description for document no. 2764, for instance, mentions correspondence from the central government (Francia and C.A. López) to the delegado of Itapúa regarding the Brazilian agent Correa de Camara and to relations with Brazil generally before 1864. In fact, 2764 is a manuscript treatise on Paraguayan politics up to the time of the Triple Alliance War. Almost certainly penned by veteran diplomat José Falcón, it records one of the few known eyewitness accounts of the 1862 Congress that confirmed the questionable succession of Francisco Solano López to the presidency of Paraguay. It is, thus, a far more important document than the meager entry would suggest. This underscores the fact that researchers owe the Gondra Collection an on-the-spot inspection, rather than just an examination of the *Calendar's* contents.

Lyndon Baines Johnson Library
2313 Red River Street
Austin, Texas 78705

---

114. Lyndon Baines Johnson Presidential Papers

Within the Johnson Library is the National Security File (NSF), Country File, Latin America. Box 72 holds Paraguayan material, including extensive correspondence on President Alfredo Stroessner's official 1968 visit to the United States. Box 1 contains a 1964 Survey of Latin America in which Paraguay receives nine pages. The NSF — Special Heads of State, Box 45, contains material addressing the then President of Paraguay, General Alfredo Stroessner. The White House Central Files (WHCF) —Subject File, Box 61 — CO 233 Paraguay also contains material touching upon President Stroessner and Paraguay. The White House Central File, Confidential File, Box 11 also hold material upon CO 233 Paraguay. In Box 17 of the President's Appointment File (Diary Backup), is a report concerning a 1965 meeting between President Johnson and the Foreign Minister of Paraguay, Raúl Sapena Pastor; and in Box 93 of the same file is further material relative to the visit of President Stroessner to the United States in 1968. Scattered throughout general material on Latin America in other files of this library are references to Paraguay, but an investigator interested in Paraguay will have do a topic by topic search. Some restrictions yet apply on the material concerning Paraguay.

115. Drew Pearson Papers

Box G 292 of this collection contains material on Paraguay collected by this prominent Washington journalist.

UTAH

Genealogical Society of Utah
Family History Department
35 N.W. Temple Street
Salt Lake City, Utah 84150

116. Archivo General de la Nación (Buenos Aires)

Several pieces touching upon Paraguay have been microfilmed from the Archivo General de la Nación in Buenos Aires:

> Indice del censo argentino, población terrestre: ejército de operaciones en el Paraguay, 1869;
>
> Indice de nombres geográficos y etnográficos del virreinato del Río de la Plata; and Catálogo de nombres y materias: fichero general, 1544-1880.

117. Archivo Nacional de Asunción

Five volumes of the Archivo Nacional de Asunción have also been microfilmed; they are of the Sección Histórica, volumes 130, 181, and 280-282.

118. Church Records of Paraguay

In the early 1970s genealogists associated with the Church of Jesus Christ of the Latter Day Saints began microfilming a series of little-known Paraguayan church records. The materials microfilmed included not only documents from the Archivo de la Curia Metropolitana in Asunción, but also from the smaller church archives in

Concepción, Villarrica, and elsewhere in the Archdiocese of Asunción. In the main, they consist of parish registers of baptisms, confirmations, marriages and deaths.

Today the microfilms form the bulk of the Paraguayan holdings of the Church's Genealogical Society of Utah, located in Salt Lake City. The Genealogical Society has the distinction of being the primary institution in the United States for the study of population changes in Paraguay. Historical demographers will find the Utah holdings fascinating. The records microfilmed mainly date from the nineteenth and early twentieth centuries, although documents sometimes do go back as far as the mid-1700s, as in the cases of Asunción and Luque. The demographic impact of the Triple Alliance War has been the subject of much speculation, but little hard data has as yet come to light. The Salt Lake City repository may provide the answer.

The collection of Paraguay church documents is the focal point of the Genealogical Society's efforts. The different documents microfilmed vary considerable in terms of historical value, completeness, and legibility. Yet even the smallest parishes are represented.

119. Aurelio Garcindo Fernandes de Sá Papers

A most curious item, rather out of place in a library devoted to genealogical themes, is a microfilmed collection of personal papers, clipping, service records, and citations concerning Aurelio Garcindo Fernandes de Sá, a Brazilian naval officer who served in Battle of Riachuelo during the 1864-1870 war with Paraguay.

120. German Federal Archive

The Society's holdings will also interest anyone pursuing research on European minorities in Paraguay. In addition to some unusual published works, this body possesses microfilms of records from the German Federal Archive at Koblenz dealing with German speaking emigrants from Russia (Mennonites) to Paraguay.

A guide to the above holdings is available in any branch library of the Genealogical Society. The microfilm records themselves are available on inter-library loan through any of the branch libraries.

VIRGINIA

Virginia Historical Society
428 North Boulevard
Richmond, Virginia 23221

121. Minor Family Papers

Robert Dabney Minor (1827-1871) of Fauquier County, Virginia, was a career naval officer. He served first with the U.S. Navy and subsequently with the Confederate Navy (in the James River Squadron). During the 1840s and 1850s Minor visited the world, calling on ports in France, China, Haiti, Mexico, and Nicaragua. At the end of the latter decade he participated in the naval expedition sent by Washington against the government of Carlos Antonio López as a response to an unprovoked Paraguayan attack on the U.S. steamer *Water Witch*. Minor, for his part, kept up a considerable correspondence with his relatives throughout this time and some of these letters (as well as some peripheral materials) touch on his Paraguayan experiences. In 1948 his family donated his entire collection of papers to the Virginia Historical Society where today they can be consulted by interested scholars. (MS 81-912)

WASHINGTON, D. C.

Agency for International Development POL/CDIE/DI
AID Development Information Center
Room 105
1601 North Kent Street
Arlington, Virginia

122. AID Development Information Center (DIC)

This center offers a variety of resources that focus on U. S. foreign assistance and international economic and social development. The DIC collection includes AID documents from the inception of this program, as well as more than 400 journal and newsletter subscriptions. All materials may be accessed using CD-ROM technology and a computerized library catalog. Materials include program and project documents covering AID's programs in Paraguay. as well as its predecessor agencies as far back as the Institute of Inter-American Affairs.

Organization of American States
Columbus Memorial Library
Constitution Avenue and 19th Street, NW
Washington, D. C. 20006

123. Columbus Memorial Library

The Columbus Memorial Library is the official library and depository for the Organization of American States, and its predecessor, the International Bureau of the American Republics and the Pan American Union. As such, it contains a wealth of material relative to Paraguay's participation in these international organizations. The library contains a complete collection of the printed documentation of these organizations as well as the *Official Records* of the OAS and *Technical Reports*. Available in the library are excellent guides to the official documents as well as the library's public card catalog.

The library also contains specialized collections, many with reference to Paraguay. Among these are holdings of the Pan American Health Organization, the Inter-American Children's Institute, the Inter-American Commission of Women, the Pan American Institute of Geography and History, the Inter-American Indian Institute, and the Inter-American Institute for Cooperation on Agriculture. While much of the material in the specialized collections is in published form, within the publications themselves are many documents touching upon activities in the American republics, including, of course, Paraguay.

Member states issue official gazettes that include information relative to laws, various types of government regulations, treaties, executive orders, etc. The library holds a comprehensive collection of these. At the same time, the library is also a depository for the United Nations and receives that body's official documentation in both Spanish and English. Such material from the UN is arranged according to that organization's cataloging system. The library has printed indices and bibliographies, as well as the public card catalog, to guide researcher through UN documentation.

An interesting holding of the Columbus Memorial Library and one of great use to researchers dealing with the international ramifications of the Chaco War is the League of Nations Collection. Printed indices and the public card catalog aid interested researchers.

Official papers, reports and publications from other international organizations are found in the library. Those bodies range from the International Labor Office, the Inter-American Development Bank, the Food and Agricultural Organization, the International Monetary Fund, the Organization for Economic Cooperation and Development, as well as a host of others. Again, interested researchers can use this material through the library's public card catalog.

Finally, one of the treasure troves of this library and absolutely necessary for any study of Paraguay's relation to the Pan American Union and the OAS is the Archives Collection. The Library and Records Management Center contained the most important collection of papers documenting the history and programs of the OAS and its predecessors. Many such papers are retrieved by means of the public card catalog or by recourse to the transmittal slips received when the papers were transferred from various offices of the General Secretariat to the archive. This collection literally holds millions of pages of printed and typewritten material.

The Columbus Memorial Library has published a large numbers of research guides to its holdings to aid investigators.

Commerce Department
Census Bureau Library
Wing 4, Room 2451
Federal Office Building 3
Suitland Road and Silver Hill Road
Suitland, Maryland

124. Census Bureau Library

This library contains one of the finest collections of national censuses of Latin America, along with scattered provincial censuses. It is particularly strong in the period after 1930. One of its outstanding holdings is the on-going International Population Census microfilm series that attempts to record every Latin American census since about 1950. It also contains central bank reports, U.S. Census Bureau's population estimates and predictions. For the recent demographic history of Paraguay this library will be of great use. There are three different card catalogs —one for material cataloged prior to March of 1976, one to 1980, and one after.

Commerce Department Library
Room 7046
14th Street and Constitution Avenue, NW
Washington, D. C. 20230

125. Commerce Department Library

In this library are some scattered documentary holdings such as reports and statistical bulletins of economic and commercial agencies, bureaus, etc., of Latin American governments. There also are some research reports and country studies by such organizations as the World Bank, the OAS, and other international bodies. Materials range back to the turn of the century and some will prove useful in any study of the Paraguayan economy and commerce.

Education Department
Educational Research Library
Room 101
555 New Jersey Avenue, NW
Washington, D. C. 20208

126. Educational Research Library

Within this library are scattered Paraguayan Ministry of Education reports and copies of that nation's laws pertaining to education.

Federal Reserve System
Research Library of the Board of Governors
Room B-C 241
20th Street and Constitution Avenue, NW
Washington, D. C. 20551

127. Federal Reserve Board Research Library

The Federal Reserve Board's Research Library holds extensive material on Latin American banking, finance, and monetary policy. Aside from the extensive periodical section, there is documentary material on central bank annual reports and bank superintendent reports, both dating from the 1920s. There are also scattered holdings of government financial reports, foreign trade reports, and national development reports. In addition, there are various reports from the 1920s onward dealing with the international financial and monetary commissions in Latin America. This library is useful for anyone studying the economic or monetary history of Paraguay in the twentieth century.

Georgetown University
Mark Joseph Launinger Library
Special Collections Division
37th and O Streets, NW
Washington, D. C. 20057

128. The George Schwarz Collection

In the Special Collections Division is housed this bound volume of Jesuit mission reports, primarily from Brazil and Paraguay from the era 1675 to 1682. These reports are useful for any study on the Jesuit experience in the Paraguayan region. A guide exists.

129. Paraguayan Jesuit Collection

In the Special Collections Division of this library are some 24 documents, most of them originals, ranging in date from 1639 to about 1744. Their major emphasis is on the struggle between the Jesuits in the Río de la Plata, and their antagonists within the Church and the civil government. Few of these have ever been used by scholars. A very explicit guide exists.

Human Rights Watch/Americas
1522 K Street, NW
Suite 910
Washington, D. C. 20005

130. Americas Watch

This organization monitors human rights violations in the Americas and elsewhere. The Americas Watch section of Human Rights Watch possesses extensive documentation upon violations committed in the era of President Alfredo Stroessner (1954-1989), not only upon the civil population of Paraguay, but also upon that nation's indigenous peoples. Material is categorized by country, and at present most of the Stroessner era documentation is in storage. Scholars should obtain prior permission from Americas Watch before investigation.

Inter-American Commission on Human Rights
8th Floor
1889 F Street, NW
Washington, D. C. 20006

131. Inter-American Commission on Human Rights

This consultative body of the OAS maintains a reference collection of human rights documents dealing with Latin America. While individual case records are confidential, the official reports to the OAS are open to investigators. These documents will be useful for an investigation into human rights violations in Paraguay during the era of Alfredo Stroessner. One should arrange an appointment to peruse the available reports.

Inter-American Commission of Women (CIM)
Room 1880
889 F. Street, NW
Washington, D. C. 20006

132. Inter-American Commission of Women

The Inter-American Commission of Women is an advisory body of the OAS. In its Washington office it holds a specialized reference collection of commission documents, proceedings of conferences, and studies. Material touching upon the status of women in Paraguay since the late 1930s may be found in these documents — particularly in the country biennial status reports. The document section, unfortunately, is not well cataloged, but the staff will aid investigators. Researchers are permitted to use the document collection but should get in touch with the CIM first.

Inter-American Development Bank
Inter-American Development Bank (IDB) Library
1300 New York Avenue, NW
Washington, D. C. 20572

133. Inter-American Development Bank

This library, aside from its fine collection of secondary sources on Latin American economics, is also a repository of IDB publications and program descriptions of bank-funded projects. Texts of Paraguayan national development plans are available on microfiche. In addition, the library receives official gazettes from every Latin American country, including, of course, Paraguay. The Bank's law library contains Paraguay legal codes, commercial financial legislation, and treaties relating to economic matters. The library publishes a quarterly *Bulletin* listing new arrivals by nation and by subject. It is open to qualified researchers with permission of the IDB.

International Monetary Fund
Records Division
700 19th Street, NW
Washington, D.C. 20431

134. International Monetary Fund — Records Division

This international organization seeks to promote currency stability among its member nations. Paraguay is a member and within the Records Division of the Main Office are kept confidential reports, correspondence, working papers, and other internally generated material relevant to the IMF's relations with Paraguay. Much of this material is of a confidential nature and therefore restricted. Any scholar desirous of using these holdings should enquire in advance as to that possibility.

International Trade Commission
International Trade Commission Library
Room 300
500 E. Street, SW
Washington, D. C. 20436

135. International Trade Commission

This library contains translations of all of Paraguay's customs laws, past to now. It also receives the official foreign trade serials and statistical yearbooks for that nation. An on-line catalog facilitates author, title, and subject access to holdings of this library. Appointments are necessary to use this library.

Labor Department
Labor Department Library
Room N 2439
New Department of Labor Building
200 Constitution Avenue, NW
Washington, D. C. 20210

136. Labor Department Library

Within this library are Latin American government documents and reports dealing with diverse items as labor codes, ministerial reports on labor laws and conditions, statistical surveys, government proclamations, and presidential addresses. For any survey of the Paraguayan labor scene since the 1920s, this library will be quite useful. Two card catalogs, one for material acquired before 1975, and the other since, will aid the researcher.

Library of Congress
Manuscript Division
10 First Street, SE
Washington, D. C. 20540

137. Charles T. Fahs Diary

U.S. Naval Surgeon Charles T. Fahs kept a diary for the period of September 2, 1858 to May 1, 1859 while serving upon the U.S.S. *Water Witch* in Paraná and Paraguay River waters. This diary is useful for a description of this cruise and its international ramifications.

138. Cordell Hull Papers

During the long service of Cordell Hull as Secretary of State (1933-1944), he held various conversations with Paraguay's ambassadors to the United States. In reel 31 of the microfilm edition of his papers there is a single folder comprising memorandum of these conversations for the years 1936-1944.

139. General Frank Ross McCoy Papers

Included within container 70 of these papers are reports prepared in 1929 by the Commission of Inquiry and Conciliation, Bolivia and Paraguay, that deal with this body's arbitration of the Chaco territorial dispute; a memorandum dated March 12, 1929, outlining the treaties and agreements between Paraguay and Bolivia relative to Chaco boundaries; and various press releases, telegrams, and background reports touching upon the same matter.

140. Joseph M. Toner Papers

Container 279 holds a report, "An Account of the Occurrences with the U.S. Steamer 'Water Witch' and the Paraguayans, February 1st, 1855"; a list of damages received by that ship; a list of her killed and wounded; and a newspaper clipping describing the bombardment of the U.S.S. *Water Witch* while in Paraguayan waters.

141. Woodrow Wilson Papers

Within the Executive Office File, Series Four, Case File 1008 is a small folder of correspondence and memoranda on matters pertaining to Paraguay for the years 1913 to 1919. This file is found upon reel 303 of the microfilm edition of the Wilson Papers.

National Archives and Records Service
8th Street and Pennsylvania Avenue, NW
Washington, D. C., 20408

The National Archives of the United States need little introduction to any serious researcher on the history of this nation. Indeed, this agency has often be termed the "memory of the nation." While the great amount of material in the Archives are open to researchers, on some there do exist restrictions. Most of the material relating to United States relations with Paraguay are found in this depository. In the various record groups can be found material on almost any other topic under the sun —agriculture, trade, labor, relations of Paraguay with other nations, and a host of more.

The organization of the National Archives is in numbered Record Groups and each group's title is generally self-explanatory. Record groups then may be broken down into topical sub-headings, and those sub-headings into further divisions. This is a very well catalogued archive, with varied and excellent guides.

142. U.S. Boundary and Claims Commissions and Arbitrations Records

Within this Record Group 76 under the heading of Records of International and Domestic Claims Commissions, 1795-1932, then the sub-heading, Claim against Paraguay under the Convention of 1859, one finds the claims of the Paraguay Navigation Company for damages incurred when Paraguay prevented that company from exercising its full rights for navigation of Paraguayan waters in the 1850s. Testimony, documents, inventories, etc. from the 1840s and 1850s are included.

Elsewhere in this Record Group under the heading, Records of the United States Participation in Foreign Boundary Disputes, 1870-1930, then the sub-heading, Argentinian-Paraguayan Boundary Arbitration, 1876-1878, is the documentary and published material submitted by both Paraguay and Argentina to President Rutherford B. Hayes in the contention of these two nations in the 1870s for possession of the Chaco. Of special interest is a collection of documents relative to this dispute filed by the Minister of Paraguay. This file is essential for any research on the Hayes Award. Another file in the same heading is the Commission of Inquiry and Conciliation: Bolivia and Paraguay, 1929-1930. That commission, appointed by the International Conference of American States on Conciliation and Arbitration, dealt with the dispute between Paraguay and Bolivia over the Gran Chaco. The United States had a seat upon this commission. Within this file are maps, printed material, and documents to support Paraguay's and Bolivia's respective claims, counter-claims, and rebuttals. This file is well indexed.

143. U.S. Bureau of Agricultural Economics Records

In this Record Group 83 under General Correspondence of the Bureau of Markets and Bureau of Agricultural Economics, 1912-1952, is some correspondence on Paraguayan agricultural and pastoral exports. In the General Correspondence of the Division of Statistical and Historical Research, 1917-1946, are statistics for Paraguayan cotton and cattle production during these years.

144. U.S. Bureau of Animal Husbandry Records

Records of this Bureau (Record Group 17) relating to Latin America are generally concerned with preventing the importation into the United States of diseased livestock and/or meat products. Paraguay supplied little, if any, cattle products to North America before the 1940s and thus little correspondence with that nation is included here. Still, under Central Correspondence, 1907-1913, File 196, there is a copy of the treaty between Argentina and Paraguay regulating the livestock trade between those two nations.

145. U.S. Bureau of Foreign and Domestic Commerce Records

Record Group 151 contains the papers of this bureau and its Latin American Division that offered to North American businessmen the best information about the commerce of Latin America. In the File on General and Miscellaneous Matters, under General Records, 1914-1945, is material relative to the commercial laws of Paraguay. Under Commodities, and Agriculture, Foods, and Forestry, are reports pertaining to Paraguay. Trade Promotion contains in a sub-section, Foreign Trade Statistics-Exports and Imports, detailed information on Paraguay's trade while the file War, contains material on German interests in Paraguay during World War I. This group is quite useful for business conditions in Paraguay in the 1920s through the 1940s.

146. U.S. Bureau of Naval Personnel Records

This Record Group 24 contains many log books of the United States Navy, among which are those of the *Water Witch* under the command of Lt. Thomas Jefferson Page of the Paraná-Paraguay river expedition of the early 1850s. They are No. 5, January 12, 1853-December 31, 1854; No. 6, January 1-December 31, 1855; and No. 7, January 1-May 12, 1856.

147. U.S. Bureau of Public Roads

Within the General Correspondence File indexed under Paraguay of this Record Group 30 are reports on roads and road construction in that nation for the 1940s.

148. U.S. Department of Commerce General Records

Within the General Correspondence of the Department, 1903-1950 of this Record Group 40 is various correspondence and statistics relating to commerce with, or foreign aid to, various Latin American nations. There is useful information on these topics pertaining to Paraguay scattered among the documentation. Some restrictions yet apply on the use of this material — particularly that of confidential business information of private firms.

149. U.S. Department of State Diplomatic Instructions

In this Record Group 59 under General Instructions are copies of instructions from the State Department to diplomats in Latin America. For Paraguay there exists one volume for the years 1858-1874. In the late 1800s the North American Minister to Uruguay also served as the Minister to Paraguay. Therefore, many instructions relative to Paraguay are found in the two volumes on Uruguay for 1867-1906. These are available on microfilm.

Under Diplomatic Despatches, 1789-1906, is the correspondence from North American diplomats in Asunción. Not only are the official communications found here, but newspapers, news clippings, pamphlets, and even private correspondence that touch on important issues are included. This material is of great importance for a study of the relations between the two nations. The Diplomatic Despatches for Paraguay comprise the years 1858-1906 and are available on microfilm.

In Records of Special Missions, 1823-1906, are instructions to special agents in the service of the United States. There, under the heading, Paraguay, are the instructions to Edward A. Hopkins, Special Agent in Asunción in the 1840s. In 1853 Lieutenant Thomas Jefferson Page, Robert C. Schenck (United States Minister to Brazil), and John S. Pendleton (Charge d'Affaires in Buenos Aires) were instructed to conclude a treaty with Paraguay. And in 1854, Charles Buckalow received orders to carry despatches to Lt. Page — the latter then on the rivers of the Río de la Plata. These records are available on microfilm.

In Records of Special Agents, 1794-1906, are found, under Paraguay, the communications of Edward A. Hopkins, Special Agent to Asunción. His correspondence deals with the political and economic conditions in Paraguay in the

1840s and 1850s and is found in volume 13 of this series. Despatches from Thomas Jefferson Page, commander of the *Water Witch* in the early 1850s, are found in volume 19, and touch mainly upon the exchange of ratification of a treaty between the United States and Paraguay. There also is in volume 19 a communication from Charles Buckalow relative to the exchange of ratification of the aforementioned treaty. These records are available on microfilm.

Notes From Foreign Missions, 1789-1906, contains the correspondence from foreign embassies and legations in the United States that was delivered to the State Department. This series is vital for an understanding of the views of Latin American nations in their diplomatic relations with the United States. In this series under Paraguay, are two volumes, 1853-1869 and 1889-1906. Both are available on microfilm.

Notes to Foreign Missions, 1793-1906, contains replies from the State Department to foreign embassies and legations in the United States. This series should be utilized in conjunction with the preceding Notes From Foreign Missions, 1789-1906. Within this series is one volume, Paraguay, 1876-1905. However, certain communications from Paraguayan representatives in the United States are found in the volume Uruguay and Paraguay, 1834-1906. This series is available on microfilm.

The series, Instructions to Consuls, 1801-1906, holds the copies of correspondence from the Department of State to United States Consuls abroad. Communications to the Consul in Paraguay are found scattered throughout this series. Various indices aid the scholar in ascertaining the location of those instructions pertaining to Paraguay.

The series, Consular Despatches, 1789-1906, deals mainly with commerce and the protection of United States citizens and their interests abroad. In this series is found, Asunción, 1844-1906. These records are useful for scholars dealing with economic conditions within Paraguay during this era. Available on microfilm.

Reports of Bureau Officers, 1790-1911, holds in volume 6 (1850-1888) an internal memorandum relative to the non-ratification of a treaty between the United States and Paraguay in the early 1850s, the claim of the United States and Paraguay Navigation Company versus the government of Carlos Antonio López in the same decade, and an account of the Paraguayan attack upon the *Water Witch*.

Within Consular Political Reports, 1925-1935, are reports from Consuls relative to important political events in the nation to which they were accredited. Often copies of these are also found in the central decimal files. This decade was an eventful one for Paraguay and analyses of political events in that republic are here.

Scattered throughout Miscellaneous Letters and Related Materials, 1789-1906, are letters from private citizens to the State Department relating to Paraguay. All letters are arranged chronologically in this series. However, there are some chronological finding guides. This series is available on microfilm.

Central Files, 1906 —, contain the bulk of State Department records for the twentieth century. In 1906 that department changed its method of filing records and to 1910 all correspondence and internally generated material were arranged by subject in a numerical series. In 1910 that single numerical series system was terminated and a new decimal system of subject classification was inaugurated. Records now are divided into major subject such as claims, extraditions, protection of interests, etc. The first digit of a document places it in a certain major category. The next two digits designate the country. Further numbers to the right of a decimal point narrow down even more explicitly the topics discussed within the document. For researchers interested in a specific topic, this new system is a great boon, as both external as well as internal State Department correspondence are now included together.

There are finding guides to the Central Files. One such is a collection of cards referring to correspondence with United States missions in various capitals, or interested agencies in the United States government. The cards labeled State Department are especially noteworthy as they often refer to policy matters.

Other card indices list names of people, companies, etc. with reference also to their decimal location. The other useful guide is a series of State Department volumes known as Purport Files. Documents were listed in chronological order, as they were filed, and described briefly by subject in accordance with the decimal system.

The above is a major source for any topic upon Paraguay in the twentieth century. Paraguayan scholars, such as Alfredo Seiferheld, have used this group. Of course, there exist some restrictions to the use of documents. Microfilm is available for the Records Relating to the Internal Affairs of Paraguay, 1919-1939, the Political Relations between the United States and Paraguay, 1910-1944, and Political Relations between Paraguay and Other States, 1930-1944.

Applications and Recommendations for Office, 1797-1901, hold the correspondence touching upon positions in the Department of State. These documents are quite useful for the background to an applicant. The records are alphabetically arranged by name of the person considered for the post, within time spans that in a general manner correspond to the years of presidential administrations. Some material on applicants to Paraguayan posts is found here.

150. U.S. Department of State Foreign Service Posts Records

This Record Group 84 holds the internal records of Latin American Embassies, Legations, and Consular posts. The material therein is quite varied, ranging from diplomats' diaries, powers of attorney, invoices, contracts, etc. The Diplomatic Post Records for Paraguay encompass the era 1861-1935. Consular Post Records for Asunción encompass the period 1887-1961. While little used, these records are essential for an understanding of the day-to-day business of diplomatic personnel abroad. Some restrictions on their use applies.

151. U.S. Foreign Agricultural Service Records

This service represents the Department of Agriculture in matters pertaining to foreign agriculture. There are various portions of this Record Group 166 that contain material relative to Paraguayan agriculture. The segment, Narrative Agricultural Reports, 1904-1954, includes reports from United States representatives abroad on every imaginable aspect of agriculture. Records are categorized in five different time periods and within each period, alphabetically by nation. Paraguay is well represented. In the segment, Forestry Reports on Central and South America, countries are listed alphabetically under a heading for South America. Within Paraguay's files are reports on the production of kapok for the 1920s and 1930s.

152. U.S. Foreign Broadcast Intelligence Service Records

This World War II Record Group 262 contains reports on, summaries of, and analyses of propaganda and news broadcasts to Latin America Europe and Japan in the years 1941 through 1946, as well as broadcasts that originated in Latin America itself. These records are useful for a study of wartime attitudes of the Axis powers toward Latin America, as well as Allied attempts to influence public opinion in that region. Under Paraguay is found a chronological index for broadcasts touching upon that nation between 1941 and 1945.

153. U.S. Foreign Economic Administration Records

Record Group 169 comprises the papers of this World War II agency that was charged with the coordination of United States government activities relative to foreign economies and economic affairs. Within the Records of the Pan American Branch, 1941-1946, are records relative to economic missions to Latin America, and correspondence with embassies as well as material upon controlled exports from the

United States to make sure that such exports did not fall into unauthorized hands. Within this file are reports on Paraguayan economic conditions and wartime foreign trade. Most material relating to Paraguay is found in the River Plate Division, 1943-1945.

154. U.S. General Accounting Office Records

There is not much in this Record Group 217 relative to Paraguay but under file, Navy Accounts, 1800-1913, are the accounts of Lt. Thomas Jefferson Page of the *Water Witch*, and the paymaster of George W. Clarke, of the *Harriet Lane*, both accounts dealing with expenditures of public money during the Paraguay-Paraná river expedition of the 1850s.

155. U.S. Headquarters Army Service Forces Records

Within this Record Group 160 are World War II records relative to the construction of air bases in Latin America — Paraguay included — as well as correspondence of the International Division, 1941-1942 touching upon lend-lease activities. Files for nations are in alphabetical order.

156. U.S. House of Representatives Records

Similar to those records of the United States Senate, the House of Representatives Record Group 233 contains much material on Latin America. For Paraguay, for instance, there are files on the *Water Witch* episode, the War of the Triple Alliance, and investigations into human rights abuses in the twentieth century. Unfortunately, the indices for House records are not as helpful as those of the Senate, but anyone studying United States-Paraguayan relations should take advantage of this record group.

157. U.S. Hydrographic Office Records

Within the file Field Notes of Exploring and Surveying Expeditions of this Record Group 37 are journals of various officers who participated in the *Water Witch* expedition of 1853-1854. Lt. Ammen contributed a "Reference Journal" and his "Notebook No. 2". Lt. Powell penned "Paraguay." A Lt. Murdaugh left us "Steamer Pilcomayo: Rios Paraguay, Confuso and Salida, Feb. 1854." Other accounts treat such varied topics as yerba mate and the *Water Witch* expedition itself. These accounts are useful for an understanding of Paraguay in the 1850s, village life, customs, etc. This file has the logs of the United States Navy ships that comprised the 1859 punitive expedition to Paraguay.

158. U.S. International Conferences, Commissions, and Expositions Records

In this Record Group 43, the file Records Relating to International Conferences of American States, 1889-1938, is really relative to the United States participation. However, some committee records, records of plenary sessions, and indices of programs of the conferences to refer to matters in which Paraguay was interested.

The Inter-American High Commission Records, 1916-1933, relate to an organ of the Pan American Union dealing with economic matters. This commission collected reports on financial and economic conditions in Latin American republics — including Paraguay — and the public debt of all Latin American nations. The purpose of this commission was to improve commercial relations among the Americas. Correspondence with Paraguay, as well as with other Latin American nations, dealt with matters of copyright, bills of exchange, and company law. Some correspondence from private firms in Paraguay is included. Within these records can be found the policy of Paraguay in reference to world trade.

The Records Relating to the International Conference of American States on Conciliation and Arbitration, 1928-1929, contain material on the policy of arbitration of difficulties between nations in this hemisphere. Within this file is material relative to the Bolivia-Paraguay Chaco dispute (particularly the armed clash at Fortín Vanguardia).

The Records Relating to the Pan-American Trade Mark Conference, 1929, has some minor material relative to Paraguay's position on trade marks.

The Records Relating to the Fifth Pan-American Commercial Conference, 1935, contains material on smuggling, ports, customs duties, classification of merchandise, tourism, etc. Within it are statements of Paraguay's policies on this matters.

The Records Relating to the Interamerican Conference for the Maintenance of Peace Held at Buenos Aires, 1936, is useful for anyone studying the termination of the Chaco War. While records of the Chaco Peace Conference itself are found elsewhere, this file holds records of the United States concern about such conflicts in Latin America, and State Department correspondence and memorandums that refer to the Chaco conflict — as well as some unofficial correspondence of Secretary of State Cordell Hull.

159. U.S. Naval Observatory Records

Within this Record Group 78 is correspondence from Lt. Thomas J. Page to Mathew Fontaine Maury, Head of the Naval Observatory, when the former commanded the *Water Witch* expedition. Most letters deal with the political situation faced by Lt. Page in Argentina and Paraguay and are valuable for personal impressions and understanding of the events that faced Lt. Page.

160. U.S. Office of Foreign Assets Control Records

This World War II office, Record Group 265, that took information on foreign-owned assets in the United States also in 1943 ordered individuals, corporations, and nominees in this country to report on property owned in foreign nations. In Series B for the year 1943-1945 are found such records for Paraguay. The Secretary of the Treasury still places severe restrictions on their use. However in 1946 the Treasury Department published *Census of American-Owned Assets in Foreign Countries* that summarized much of the information gathered. One may find this report in the Library of the National Archives.

161. U.S. Office of Inter-American Affairs Records

Record Group 229 contains the papers of this office that was an emergency creation during World War II. Its life was relatively brief, 1940-1946. It existed to promote United States economic and cultural programs in Latin America, and to combat Axis influence there. It also served as a coordinating and advisory agency for most other government bodies dealing with Latin America. On the conclusion of the war, many of its records were passed to other government agencies. However, the Records Relating to Basic Economy and Development Programs, 1940-1945, contain much material on economic topics, arranged by country. Paraguay is represented here. The same is true of Records Relating to Transportation, 1940-1947. Within this file, arranged by country, there are useful and detailed reports on Paraguay's land and river transportation in the era of World War II.

162. U.S. Office of Naval Records and Library Naval Records

In this Record Group 45 is the Records of the Office of the Secretary of the Navy holding the series, Letters from Officers Commanding Squadrons, 1841-1886. In the latter is the correspondence of the South Atlantic Squadron. The volume for 1858-1859 contains the letters of Commodore W. B. Shubrick during the punitive expedition to Paraguay of those years and is useful for researchers looking into the entire *Water Witch* episode of the 1850s. Much correspondence in this series for the 1860s concerns the Paraguayan war. Questions addressed were the conduct of the war, the efficacy of the Brazilian blockade, and the United States Navy's interjection into the diplomatic controversies surrounding the relations of Minister to Asunción Charles Ames Washburn and President Francisco Solano López. This correspondence is extremely useful for a North American view of the war. Available on microfilm.

Also within the Records of the Office of the Secretary of the Navy, under the series Letters from Officers Commanding Expeditions, 1818-1855, is the correspondence of Lieutenant Thomas Jefferson Page, commander of the *Water Witch* when in the 1850s he was engaged in the exploration and mapping of the Paraná and Paraguay rivers. It is bound in a volume titled "Letters &c. from Lt. T. J. Page, commanding U.S. Steamer Water Witch: Exploration and Survey of the Rivers La Plata, Paraguay and Parana and their Tributaries. January 6, 1853 and August 4, 1856." This correspondence to the Secretaries of the Navy John Kennedy and James Dobbin is quite complete as Page reported on port facilities, tributaries of the main rivers, political conditions, and a host of other geographical, political, and commerce topics. This correspondence is essential for an understanding of the *Water Witch* controversy. This series is available on microfilm.

Within the series Letters from Officers below the Rank of Commander, 1802-1884, also in the Records of the Office of Secretary of the Navy is further correspondence of Lieutenant Thomas Jefferson Page relative to the *Water Witch* expedition. This series also is available on microfilm.

Under Papers Acquired from Private Sources, is Letter Books of Officers of the United States Navy, 1778-1908. The latter contains the correspondence of Rear Admiral Charles H. Davis, who commanded the South Atlantic Squadron in the late 1860s. In the two volumes of letters to the Secretary of Navy, that officer submitted his views on affairs in the Río de Plata during the Paraguayan War. He also reports on his conversation with Francisco Solano López held in Paraguay during the U.S. Navy expedition up the Paraguay River during the war itself.

163. U.S. Office of Price Administration Records

This World War II office was responsible for wartime price stabilization. Some of its activities included cooperation with American nations in the control of import and export prices. Various reports within this Record Group 188 deal with Latin America, such as an extensive wartime report on Paraguayan yerba mate found in the Imported Foods Section.

164. U.S. Office of War Administration Records

This office was a World War II agency established in 1942 for the furtherance of propaganda against the Axis. Very few of its activities concerned Latin America as that region was in the hands of the Office of the Coordinator of Inter-American Affairs. Nonetheless, there is some material pertaining to Paraguay in this Record Group 209. Within the file, Latin America — Pacific world-informational file, 1941-1946, that constitutes part of the Regional Analysis Division of the Bureau of Overseas Intelligence is a 1943 typescript concerning medical and sanitation information on Paraguay, and an eleven page report in 1944 prepared by R. Henry Rowntree, "Transportation in Paraguay."

165. U.S. Post Office Department Records

In this Record Group 28 under Postal Conventions with Foreign Countries, 1856-1929, then under Paraguay are postal conventions and agreements between the United States and that republic.

166. U.S. Public Health Service Records

Record Group 90 contains the records of this agency that protects the health of Americans and also cooperates with foreign governments and international organizations in world health activities. Within the various segments dealing with material on quarantine stations outside the United States for the Twentieth Century (1897—) are various files designated Foreign Stations and those for 1924-1935, and 1936-1944, contain correspondence between the Public Health Service and Paraguayan officials, as well as private citizens, on various health issues. Each Latin American government has its own file. There also is some minor correspondence with Paraguay relative to Pan American Sanitary Conferences in the first half of the twentieth century.

167. U.S. Reconstruction Finance Corporation Records

This New Deal Agency, Record Group 234, gave aid to various parts of the United States economy and in World War II acquired strategic material for war purposes. It had a wide range of economic and financial operations in Latin America. Within the Records of the United States Commercial Company, 1942-1951, are various wartime records dealing with Paraguay and that nation's products that were important to the Allies. Some restrictions yet apply on certain records of the RFC.

168. U.S. Senate Records

Senate records (Record Group 46) contain many documents relative to the international relations of the United States. Among them may be found documents ranging from North American difficulties with Paraguay during the Triple Alliance War (1864-1870) to questions of human rights abuses during the regime of General Alfredo Stroessner (1954-1989). Also in this group is correspondence relative to consular diplomatic post nominations. This group is well indexed but certain restrictions on its use apply.

169. U.S. Shipping Board Records

From World War I to 1933 this board (Record Group 32) regulated United States carriers and encouraged the United States Merchant Marine. Given Paraguay's land-locked status and the paucity of direct maritime trade with the United States, there are only a few references to that nation in the Subject-Classified Files, 1917-1936. In the General File of the Division of Operation, 1917-1934, are some references to North American firms operating in Paraguay.

170. U.S. War Department General and Special Staffs Records

In the Military Intelligence Division, 1917-1941, file of this Record Group 165 are reports from United States Military Attaches in Latin America. For this file there is a country registry that permits a researcher to find particular reports quite readily. Reports on Paraguay, of course, are included. Among the records of the Office of the Director of Plans and Operations, Pan-American Group is material relevant to the defense of Latin America during World War II and reports dealing with the construction of Latin American air bases. The latter was an important issue in North American wartime relations with Paraguay. The records of the Military Intelligence Service, Latin American Branch, 1940-1946, contain interesting reports on the condition of, as well as the political-ideological attitudes then current in the Paraguayan Army. Given the role of the army in the political direction of that republic since the 1930s, this record group is of great value for anyone studying political-military relations in that nation.

171. U.S. Weather Bureau Records

This Record Group 27 holds a few weather records for Asunción in the mid 1850s.

National Geographic Society
National Geographic Society Archives
17th and M Streets, N.W.
Washington, D. C. 20036

172. National Geographic Society

In the past the National Geographic Society has sponsored scientific research involving Paraguay. Some of those research projects have been reported in the society's *Research and Exploration*. While all scientists so sponsored are required to file reports on their projects with the society, unfortunately at present these reports are only available for review with special permission from a Society official.

Catholic University of America
The Oliveira Lima Library
620 Michigan Avenue, NE
Washington, D.C. 20064

173. The Manoel de Oliveira Lima Collection

Born in Brazil and educated in Portugal, Manoel de Oliveira Lima (1867-1928) was a Renaissance man with an international reputation in diplomacy and journalism. Early in life he developed an interest in collecting rare books, pamphlets, and documents. By the time of his retirement, he had assembled one of the world's finest collections of materials on Brazil, Portugal, and the Lusophone world. Dr. Oliveira Lima donated his library to the Catholic University in 1916, and since the mid-1920s its thousands of manuscripts, more than 50,000 printed items, and many pieces of art and memorabilia has rested in the bottom floor of the John K. Mullen Library building.

Although Paraguay was never the focus of Dr. Oliveira Lima's collecting, he did manage to acquire a few items incidentally, some of them very unusual indeed. Take, for example, Codex no. 84 — Antonio Ribeiro Sanches (1699-1783), "Discursos sobre a America Portuguesa": written in 1763 by an exiled Sephardic physician, this manuscript was one of the first written in Brazil proper that, among other things, attempted to thoughtfully analyze the communitarian system of the Jesuit Order in Paraguay.

Other documents include: Sousa Correia Papers, nos. 59-61, which concern Brazilian rearmament in the wake of the Empire's victory over Paraguay in 1870; a September 1865 letter from José Inácio de Abreu e Lima to "the Barao," in which he describes the Triple Alliance War battle of Yatai (Misc. Papers no. 56); an 1839 petition addressed by merchant Caetano Doldán to Dictator José Gaspar de Francia requesting permission to dispose of some goods (Misc. Papers no. 118); and several printed items of Jesuit origin. One, the *Arte de la lengua guaraní* (published 1724) is especially curious as a notation within its cover indicates that this grammar was the personal property of Francisco Solano López; it was taken from his luggage by a Brazilian officer at the time of his death at Cerro Corá.

Since a good portion of the Oliveira Lima's holdings has never been adequately catalogued, the diligent researcher will almost certainly find interesting treasures on Paraguay, such as several rare and unusual pamphlets on the Triple Alliance War. The Library also boasts many sets of Brazilian newspapers (1850s through 1920s) as well as scores of single issues of newspapers and journals. A goodly number of these touch parenthetically on Paraguayan matters.

Organization of American States
Documentation and Information Service Library
Department of Educational Affairs
Room 200-9, 2nd Floor
General Secretariat Building
889 F. Street, NW
Washington, D. C. 20006

174. Documentation and Information Service Library

This library for the OAS Department of Educational Affairs receives publications on every aspect of Latin American education. Much of the holdings are reports, as well as publications, of the ministries of education of Latin American governments, as well as technical reports from the OAS and other international organizations such as the World Bank. The proceedings of inter-American conferences upon education are also filed here. In addition, there exist files relative to national legislation upon education that are arranged by country. The collection dates from about World War II to the present. Paraguay is well represented in this library, and any researcher doing a serious, in-depth investigation into the state of Paraguayan education in the past half-century would be well advised to utilize this library's resources. A card catalog exists to facilitate investigations.

Organization of American States
Records Management Center
Room G-6
Administrative Building
19th Street and Constitution Avenue, NW
Washington, D. C. 20006

---

175. Records Management Center/Organization of American States

The center houses the millions of documents consisting of internal staff correspondence, conference papers, and correspondence of the OAS, and its predecessor, the Pan American Union. The center also preserves the original copies of Inter-American treaties, agreements, conventions, etc. Lists of all records are available in the Center, arranged according to the office of origination and date. Anyone studying the relationship of Paraguay to the Pan American Union, and then to the OAS should utilize this center. Almost all the records of this center are open to researchers, but an appointment is recommended.

Pan American Health Organization
PAHO Library
Room 607
525 23rd Street, NW
Washington, D. C. 20037

---

176. Pan American Health Organization

This collection specializes in medical and public health literature of Latin America. Included are annual reports of public health agencies from the early twentieth century, surveys of public health and nutrition, health plans, reports on vital statistics, reports from inter-American technical conferences on health, national legislation pertaining to public health, and government documents on population and family planning. Some scattered censuses and national planning documents, as well as World Bank economic studies are also present. The library also maintains a complete collection of Pan American Health Organization official documents, country agreements, country-representative reports, and PAHO publications and technical studies. For any researcher interested in Paraguay medicine and public health, as well as family planning, this collection will be extremely useful. This library is open for research and there is an author-subject catalog to aid investigators. The internal archives of this organization are housed in the same location.

Peace Corps
Peace Corps Information Services Division Library
Room E-5353
1990 K Street, NW
Washington, D. C. 20526

177. Peace Corps Library

Paraguay, from the early days of Peace Corps, has witnessed a strong in-country effort by this program. In this library are documents dealing with such diverse matters as programs, reports on projects in Paraguay, evaluations of those programs, and volunteers' newsletters. A card catalog under country headings is available.

United States Information Agency
United States Information Agency Library
Room 315
301 4th Street, SW,
Washington, D. C. 20547

178. Documents Branch

Within this section of the USIA Library are millions of items from 1944 to the present. Among them are unclassified U.S. government reports and news releases, reports emanating from international organizations and agencies, and newspaper clippings. This collection is organized by geographic area, and then by subject. In addition, this branch maintains biographic files on major Latin American government officials, financial figures, and cultural personages. This collection will be of use to any researcher surveying the state of Paraguayan-United States relations over the past half century. There is an index available.

179. Propaganda Collection

This collection is mainly devoted to Communist propaganda, books, magazines, leaflets, pamphlets, etc. Holdings are organized by country. The material in this collection will be of some use for anyone studying the Paraguayan Communist Party, and also for Soviet views of Paraguay since the 1960s.

Both collections are closed to the public, but qualified researchers can gain permission to some material.

U. S. State Department
State Department Library
State Department Building,
Room 3239
2201 C Street, NW
Washington, D. C. 20520

---

180. State Department Library

This library, as one might expect, is very strong in international treaty collections, including those of the United States with Paraguay. Paraguayanists will also find treaties of other foreign powers with that nation as well. The library is limited to personnel of the State Department and a few other government bodies. In cases of urgent need, however, scholars may request permission to use this library.

U.S. Treasury Department
Treasury Department Library
Room 5030
15th Street and Pennsylvania Avenue, NW
Washington, D. C. 20220

---

181. Treasury Department Library

This library receives central bank reports and official statistical bulletins from nearly all Latin American nations. It also has scattered holdings of national budgets, and reports from specialized state banks (industrial development, agricultural, pastoral, etc). Most material is post-1960 in content. This library will be useful for anyone investigating the economic policy of Paraguay during the Stroessner years.

Washington Office on Latin America (WOLA)
Suite 404
110 Maryland Avenue, NE
Washington, D. C. 20002

---

182. Washington Office on Latin America

WOLA is a public-interest group whose purpose is to observe and monitor the actions of the United States in Latin America, as well as to support democratic movements and human rights in that region. It maintains a reference collection of reports and clippings relative to Latin America organized by country. There is some useful material on Paraguay dealing with the Stroessner dictatorship and the transition to democracy.

WEST VIRGINIA

West Virginia University
Charles C. Wise Library
Colson Hall
Morgantown, West Virginia 26506

183. Mrs. Louis Bennett Papers

Mrs. Bennett's diary of a trip (cataloged as Collection no. 50) to South America around the turn of the century amounts to 150 pages of which eight are dedicated to Paraguay. The diary is interesting for its attention to detail, and especially for its glimpse of traditional life in interior towns such as Villarrica, Encarnación, and San Bernardino.

COLLECTION INDEX

Actas Capitulares del Cabildo de la Asunción. 53
AID Development Information Center. 122
Almy, John Jay. 94
Alvarado García, Ernesto. 54
Americas Watch. 130
Archivo General de la Nación/Argentina. 116
Archivo Nacional de Asunción (U of Georgia). 30
Archivo Nacional de Asunción (U of Louisville). 69
Archivo Nacional de Asunción (U of Texas). 112
Archivo Nacional de Asunción (Utah). 117
Archivum Romanum Societatis Iesu. 84

Bealer, Lewis Winkler. 3
Bender, Harold S. 36
Bennett, Mrs. Louis. 183
Board of Foreign Scholarships. 89
Board of Missions, Commission on Overseas Missions/Mennonites. 49
Boston Public Library. 75

Carter, Jimmy. 29
Census Bureau Library. 124
Chaco War (González/U of Kansas). 55
Chamberlain, Hazel. 109
Chaves, Julio César. 19
Church Records of Paraguay. 118
Columbus Memorial Library. 123

Commerce Department Library. 125
Council for International Exchange of Scholars. 1

Dag Hammarskjold Library. 92
Daily Morning Herald. 87
DeForest, David Curtis. 26
Dennis, William C. 34
Díaz Pérez, Virato. 18
Diplomacy (González/U of Kansas). 56
Documentation and Information Service/OAS. 174
Documents Branch/USIA. 178
Documents Collection (Widener Library). 77

Educational Research Library. 126
Eisenhower, Dwight D. 52
Emmons Family. 27
Evarts, William Maxwell. 105

Fahs, Charles T. 137
Federal Reserve Board Research Library. 127
Fernandes de Sá, Aurelio Garcindo. 119
Fogg, John S. H. 70
Fondo Gesuitico al Gesu. 85
Ford, Gerald. 81
Francia, Dr. José Gaspar de. 57
Freidmann, Robert. 37
Frost, Welsey. 108

General Conference of Mennonite Brethren Churches/Board of General Welfare and
        Public Relations. 8
German Federal Archive. 120
Giesbrecht, Gerhard B. 9
Godoi, Juan Silvano. 20
Goldsborough, Louis M. 100
Gondra, Manuel E. 113
González, Juan Natalicio. 58
Gordon, George J. R. 4
Government Reports (González/U of Kansas). 59
Graber, Christian L. 38

Graham, Walter B. 95
Grevstad, Nicoly Andrew. 82
Grupo Staudt. 60

Hale, Albert Barlow. 31
Hayes, Rutherford B. 106
Hickenlooper, Bourke B. 46
Hiebert, Peter C. 50
Hoover, Herbert. 47
Hull, Cordell. 138
Huntington Library/Department of Manuscripts. 13

Institute of Jesuit History. 32
Inter-American Commission on Human Rights. 131
Inter-American Commission of Women. 132
Inter-American Development Bank. 133
International Monetary Fund/Records Division. 134
International Trade Commission. 135

Johnson, Lyndon Baines. 114

Kell, John MacIntosh. 101
Kennedy, John Fitzgerald. 76

Labor Department. 136
Latin American Pamphlet Collection. 91
Latin American Political Posters. 83
Latrocinios Chavistas. 61
Libros de Real Hacienda. 62
Licht der Indianern. 10
Lima, Manoel de Oliveira. 173
Litwiller, Nelson and Ada. 39
Lohrentz, Abraham M. 51
López, Carlos Antonio. 63
Love Library/Special Collections/SDSU. 25

McCoy, General Frank Ross. 139

McCulloch, Carleton. 43
Mennonite Brethren Missions/Service/Paraguay Mission. 11
Mennonite Central Committee. 40
Minor Family. 121
Miscellaneous (González/U of Kansas). 64
Miscellaneous Holdings (UC-Riverside). 21
Morínigo, Victor. 65
Muse, Benjamin. 102

Nasatir, Abraham P. 24
National Agricultural Library. 71
National Geographic Society. 172
Nicholson, Meredith. 44
Nixon, Richard M. (Vice President). 15
Nixon, Richard M. 16, 72

Original and Copied Nineteenth Century Material (González/U of Kansas). 66

Pan American Health Organization. 176
Pamphlets Collection (Widener Library). 78
Paraguayan Jesuit Collection. 129
Pastells, P. Pablo. 86
Pearson, Drew. 115
Peace Corps. 177
Plan of Economic Development (González/U of Kansas). 67
Propaganda Collection/USIA. 179

Quiring, Walter. 42

Rare Jesuitica. 33
Ratslaff, Gerhard. 12
Reagan, Ronald. 17
Records Management Center/OAS. 175
Rich, Obadiah. 96
Río Paraguay. 68
Rockefeller Foundation. 97
Rodríguez Alcalá, Hugo. 22

Roosevelt, Franklin D. 98
Roosevelt, Theodore. 79

Schenck, Robert Cumming. 107
Schwarz, George. 128
Seventh Day Adventists. 74
Snyder, Elvin V. 41
Socialist Party of America. 103
Society of Jesus (1). 6
Society of Jesus (2). 7
Soper, Fred. 73
Sound Recordings of South American Indian Languages. 45
Southern Baptist Historical Library and Archives. 111
Steedman, Charles. 104
Stewart, William. 93

Toner, Joseph M. 140
Truman, Harry S. 88

United Nations Centre for Science and Technology for Development. 99
United States and Paraguay Navigation Company. 110
University Students (Widener Library). 80
U.S. Boundary and Claims Commissions and Arbitrations. 142
U.S. Bureau of Agricultural Economics. 143
U.S. Bureau of Animal Husbandry. 144
U.S. Bureau of Education and Cultural Affairs. 2
U.S. Bureau of Foreign and Domestic Commerce. 145
U.S. Bureau of Naval Personnel. 146
U.S. Bureau of Public Roads. 147
U.S. Department of Commerce. 148
U.S. Department of State. 149
U.S. Department of State Foreign Service Posts. 150
U.S. Department of State/Library. 180
U.S. Department of the Treasury/Library. 181
U.S. Foreign Agricultural Service. 151
U.S. Foreign Broadcast Intelligence Service. 152
U.S. Foreign Economic Administration. 153
U.S. General Accounting Office. 154
U.S. Headquarters Army Service Forces. 155
U.S. House of Representatives. 156

U.S. Hydrographic Office. 157
U.S. International Conferences, Commissions, and Expositions. 158
U.S. Naval Observatory. 159
U.S. Office of Foreign Assets Control. 160
U.S. Office of Inter-American Affairs. 161
U.S. Office of Naval Records and Library. 162
U.S. Office of Price Administration. 163
U.S. Office of War Administration. 164
U.S. Post Office Department. 165
U.S. Public Health Service. 166
U.S. Reconstruction Finance Corporation. 167
U.S. Senate. 168
U.S. Shipping Board. 169
U.S. War Department General and Specific Staffs. 170
U.S. Weather Bureau. 171

Various Papers, Manuscripts (UC-Berkeley). 5

Washington Office on Latin America. 182
Webb, James Watson. 28
Weyer, Guillermo Arturo. 23
White, Francis. 48
Williams, Sara Lockwood. 90
Willis. 14
Wilson, Woodrow. 141
Wood, Thomas Bond. 35

SUBJECT INDEX

Agencia Noticiosa Paraguaya. 23
Agriculture and Livestock. 58, 59, 71, 97, 123, 143, 144, 145, 151
Agrupación Revolucionaria de Trabajadores (Trotskyist). 23
Archivo General de la Nación (Argentina). 115
Archivo Nacional de Asunción. 20, 69, 112, 117
Argentina. 142, 144
Armed Forces. 170
Artigas, José Gervasio. 20
Asociación Nacional Republicana (Colorados). 23
Audibert, Alejandro. 20
Axis Espionage, Influence, and Propaganda (1940-1945). 23, 98, 108, 152
Ayala, Eusebio. 43
Ayala, Pacífico de. 20

Báez, Cecilio. 20, 56
Báez, Guillermo. 20
Banco Nacional (Central Bank). 61, 127
Bareiro Saguier, Rubén. 22
Bender, Harold S. 36, 40
Bender, John. 40
Bogarín, Juan Sinforiano. 20
Bolivia. 139
Bonpland, Aimé. 20
Boundaries. 34, 105, 113
Brazil. 107
Bruce, James. 88
Buckalow, Charles. 149

Caballero, Bernardino. 20
Cabildo of Asunción. 53
Cajas Reales, 1772-1788 & 1803-1811 (Royal Treasury Records). 62, 69
Calvo, Carlos. 19
Campos Cervera, Herib. 22
Cárdenas, Bernardino de. 96, 113, 129
Cárcano, Ramón J. 20
Cardozo, Efraím. 22
Casaccia, Gabriel. 22
Centurión, Juan Crisóstomo. 56, 93
Chaco.
        Dispute. 113
        Commission of Inquiry and Conciliation (1929). 47, 48, 129, 142, 158
        Hayes Arbitration Award (1878). 105, 106, 142
        Peace Conference (1935-1938). 21, 98, 158
        War (1932-1935). 19, 43, 44, 55, 64, 65, 92, 98, 103, 123
Children. 123
Chodasewicz, Rodolfo. 20
Church and Parish Records. 118
Club Atlético Deportivo Paraguayo (Buenos Aires). 23
Cold War. 52, 76, 114
Columbus Memorial Library. 123
Comité Paraguayo and British Loans. 20
Commerce. 4, 20, 31, 68, 88, 125, 127, 133, 135, 145, 148, 153, 158, 161, 162,
        163, 167
Communist Propaganda. 175
Confederación Paraguaya de Trabajadores. 23
Constitutions of Paraguay. 91
Corporación Paraguaya (Mennonite). 40
Corruption. 61
Cultural Exchanges. 2
Customs Administration. 98, 135, 158

Davis, Charles H. 162
Decoud, José Segundo. 20
Decoud, Hector Francisco. 20
Demography. 116, 118, 120, 124, 176
Development. 58, 67, 123, 127, 133, 161
Díaz Pérez, Viriato. 18
Drug Traffic. 29, 92

Education. 97, 126, 174
Eisenhower, Dwight D. 52
Emmons, George Foster. 27
Environment. 99
Estigarribia, José Félix. 3, 98
Evarts, William Maxwell. 105
Exiles. 23

Family Planning. 175
Fernandes de Sá, Aurelio Garcindo. 119
Ferreira, Benigno. 20
Ford, Gerald. 81
Foreign Relations, General. 56, 65, 180
Forestry. 151
Francia, Dr. José Gaspar de. 20, 21, 30, 57, 64, 69, 173
Franco, Rafael. 23
Freedom of the Press. 92
Frente Amplio de Mujeres. 23
Frente Unido de Liberación Nacional. 23
Frost, Wesley. 108
Fulbright Awards. 1, 2, 89

Gelly, Jaun Andrés. 56
Genealogy. 116, 118, 120
Germans in Paraguay. 120, 145
Genocide. 92
Giesbrecht, Gerhard B. 9
Godoi, Juan Silvano. 20
Godoi, Nicanor. 20
Gondra, Manuel E. 113
González, Juan Natalicio. 58
González Delvalle, Alcibiades. 23
Government Finance. 20, 59, 60, 123, 133, 134, 158, 181
Graber, Christian. 38
Graham, Walter B. 95
Grevsted, Nicolay Andrew. 82
Grupo Staudt Cartel. 60
Guanes, Alejandro. 22
Guerilla Movements. 23

Hayes, Rutherford B. 106
Health and Medicine. 20, 49, 51, 73, 97, 111, 123, 164, 166, 175
Hickenlooper, Bourke B. 46
Hiebert, Peter C. 50
Honduras. 54
Hoover, Herbert. 47
Hopkins, Edward A. 70, 110, 149
Hopkins, Harry. 98
Hull, Cordell, 107, 138, 158
Human Rights. 23, 92, 130, 131, 168, 182
Hydro-Electric Development. 99

Immigration. 3, 9, 36, 38, 39, 40, 41, 42, 49, 50, 120
Indians. 10, 11, 45, 49, 58, 92, 113, 123, 130
Inland South American Missionary Union. 109
Institute of Inter-American Affairs. 122
International Labor Organization. 92

Jesuits. 5, 6, 7, 13, 21, 32, 33, 84, 85, 86, 96, 113, 128, 129, 173
Johnson, Lyndon Baines. 114

Kennedy, John Fitzgerald. 76
Kratz, Maxwell H. 40
Kreek, George L. 47, 48

Labor. 23, 123, 136
Lamas Carísimo de Rodríguez Alcalá, Teresa. 22
Legal Code. 133
League of Nations. 123
Letelier, Orlando. 29
Literature and Culture. 18, 23, 20, 22, 64
López, Carlos Antonio. 19, 20, 21, 63, 69, 70, 101, 110
López, Francisco Solano. 19, 25, 69, 75, 93, 162
López, Juan Francisco. 20
López, Miguel Solano. 81
Lohrentz, Abraham. 51
Lynch, Eliza. 20, 93

Mann, Thomas. 52
Mennonites in the Chaco. 8, 9, 10, 11, 12, 36, 37, 38, 39, 40, 41, 42, 49, 50, 51,
        120
Mennonites in Asunción. 49
Methodists. 35
Mexico. 58
Milligan, James F. 87
Morínigo, Higínio. 65, 98
Movimiento de Liberación Nacional "14 de Mayo". 23
Movimiento Popular Colorado (Mopoco). 23

Nasatir, Abraham. 24
National Socialism. 12
Nicholson, Meredith. 43, 44
Nixon, Richard M. 15, 16, 72

O'Leary, Juan E. 20
Organization of American States (OAS). 123, 125, 174, 175
Organización Primero de Marzo. 23

Page, Thomas Jefferson. 149, 162
Pan-American Union. 98, 123, 175
Pamphlets. 19, 78, 91
Paraguay, General. 14, 26, 77, 78, 115
Paraguay River. 59, 68, 157, 162
Paraguayan History.
        Conquest and Exploration (1519-1556). 96, 113
        Colonial Era (1557-1810). 53, 69, 77, 113, 117
        Independence (1811-1816). 69, 113
        Nineteenth Century. 57, 63, 66, 112, 113
Paraguayan State Railway. 59
Paraguayo Independiente. 21
Partido Comunista Paraguayo. 23
Partido Democrata Cristiano. 23
Partido Liberal. 23
Partido Revolucionario Febrista (febristas). 23
Pastor Benítez, Justo. 22
Peasant Organizations. 23
Pendleton, John S. 149
Plá, Josefina. 22

Politics. 20, 23, 64, 113, 175, 182
Political Posters. 83
Postal Conventions. 165
Provisional Paraguayan Government (1869). 20

Reagan, Ronald. 17
Rebelión de Concepción (1947 Civil War). 23
Recalde Rodríguez de Francia, Petrona. 20
Rein, Ewald. 49
Reimer, Jacob. 49
Revolution (1873). 20
Revolutionary Plots (1870s). 20
Rivarola, Cirilo Antonio. 20
Roa Bastos, Augusto. 22
Roads and Transportation. 147, 161
Rockefeller foundation. 73, 97
Rodríguez Alcalá, Hugo. 22
Romero, Elivio. 22
Roosevelt, Franklin Delano. 91
Roosevelt, Theodore. 79
Rural Development. 99

Schenck, Robert Cumming. 107, 149
Science and Geography. 68, 113, 172
Seventh Day Adventists. 74
Shaw, George P. 88
Shubrick, William. 87, 162
Soper, Fred. 73
Southern Baptist Convention. 111
Stewart, William. 93
Stroessner, Alfredo. 23, 52, 83, 114, 130, 131, 168, 182
Student Organizations. 23

Talavera, Carmelo. 56
Talavera, Natalicio. 56
Tewksbury, Howard H. 88
Travel Accounts. 90, 100
Treaty of Madrid (1750). 7, 77, 113
Trejo y Sanabria, María de. 20
Truman, Harry S. 88

UNESCO. 92
Unión de Mujeres Paraguayas. 23
United Nations. 92, 123
United States and Paraguay Navigation Company. 110, 142
United States.
        Aid. 98, 122, 148, 153, 167
        Air Bases. 155, 170
        Assets in Paraguay. 160, 169
        Commerce. 31, 88, 145, 148, 153, 163, 167
        Development. 161
        Export-Import Bank. 52
        Foreign Relations. 15, 16, 17, 24, 29, 31, 43, 44, 46, 47, 70, 72, 81, 82,
                95, 102, 105, 106, 107, 110, 114, 138, 150, 156, 168, 175, 180
        House of Representatives. 156
        Information Agency. 178
        Military Intelligence. 170
        Peace Corps. 177
        Punitive Naval Expedition (1858-1859). 87, 94, 100, 104, 121, 149, 157,
                162
        War of Triple Alliance. 28, 75, 162, 168
        Water Witch Affair (1853-1855). 27, 110, 137, 146, 149, 154, 155, 157,
                158, 162
        Senate. 168
University Students. 23, 79
Uriarte, Higínio. 20

Village and Rural Life. 97, 109, 157, 183.

Washburn, Charles Ames. 162
War of the Triple Alliance (1864-1870). 20, 25, 28, 66, 75, 77, 113, 116, 119,
       162, 168, 173
War Refugees. 98
Warren, Fletcher. 88
Waugh, Sanauel. 52
Weather. 171
Weyer, Guillermo Arturo. 23
Wheeler, Post. 47, 48
White, Francis. 48
Wilson, Woodrow. 141
Women's Issues. 23, 123, 132
Wood, Thomas Bond. 35

Woodrow Wilson Memorial Library. 92
World Bank. 125
World Health Organization. 92
World War I. 145, 169
World War II. 108, 138, 152, 153, 155, 160, 161, 163, 164, 167, 170

Yerba Mate. 20, 113, 157, 163
Ynsfran, Pablo Max. 22

About the Authors

THOMAS WHIGHAM is Associate Professor of History at the University of Georgia. He is the author of *The Politics of River Trade: Tradition and Development in the Upper Plata, 1780–1870* (1991) and is currently writing a history of the Paraguayan War.

JERRY W. COONEY is Professor Emeritus of History at the University of Louisville. He is the author of *Economia y Sociedad en la Intendencia del Paraguay* (1990) as well as many articles.

ISBN 0-313-29203-5

90000>

EAN

9 780313 292033

HARDCOVER BAR CODE